Indra Devi

YOGA

FOR

AMERICANS

*A Complete 6 Weeks' Course
for Home Practice*

PRENTICE-HALL, INC.
ENGLEWOOD CLIFFS, N.J.

© 1959 by PRENTICE-HALL, INC., Englewood Cliffs, N.J.

Copyright under International and Pan American Copyright Conventions

All rights reserved, including the right to reproduce this book, or any portions thereof, in any form except for the inclusion of brief quotations in a review.

Library of Congress Catalog Card Number 59-11120

Printed in the United States of America

97233

To my friend and pupil
GLORIA SWANSON
for her ever-searching, burning, crusading spirit, admirable courage, keen sense of humor and luminous laughter.

Foreword

This welcome book by Indra Devi is further evidence of the interest that has been awakened in the United States, Canada, and other countries of the Western world, for the practical aspects, applicable to our own mode of living, of the ancient science of Yoga.

Yoga is one of the greatest disciplines in the world and can be practiced at each stage with positive results. It aims at controlling one's physical as well as one's spiritual and mental climate. The circulation of the blood, the degree of tension in the muscles and in the nerves, the very thoughts that enter the mind—are all subjected to progressive control.

The achievement of the final stage of bliss is beyond the conception of most mortals, even among yogis themselves, and is reached only by a few who have passed through all the stages and have proven themselves worthy by their own merits.

I can recommend Yoga wholeheartedly from my own experience. It is an unfailing source of vitality and good humor.

Let us learn a little of its philosophy and its application, just as India and all the Eastern world today are busy learning what we know and what we can teach.

YEHUDI MENUHIN

Author's Preface

HOW YOGA CAN BE OF HELP TO *YOU*

FRANKLY SPEAKING, I DID NOT INTEND TO WRITE AGAIN ON Yoga postures, since in my previous book, *Forever Young, Forever Healthy*,[1] I have already described them and spoken at length on relaxation, breathing, diet, weight control and such common complaints as tension, nervousness, insomnia, colds, headaches, constipation, asthma, arthritis, etc. . . .

In fact, I did not think that another book on this subject would be necessary. However, as soon as letters from my readers started pouring in, I found that I was wrong. A great number of people here in the United States—and elsewhere— were anxious to be given an outlined program they could follow day by day. They believed that, as beginners, they would in this way have more confidence in what they were doing and also have a feeling of being guided and taught instead of being left to themselves.

Many were also afraid of falling into the hands of charlatans and self-appointed teachers when seeking advice, since there seems to be quite a number of unscrupulous and dishonest individuals who style themselves as real yogis, but who are only

---
[1] Prentice-Hall, Inc., Englewood Cliffs, N.J., 1953.

out to exploit the name of Yoga. This type of "teacher," whether homegrown or imported (even from India), usually has only one interest in mind: to take advantage of gullible followers and extract as much money from them as possible. "We are like little birds in the nest," one such unfortunate student complained to me, "who open our beaks wide, expecting to be fed, but instead have pebbles pushed into their mouths by cruel boys who imitate the cry of the mother bird."

The desire to give a clearer understanding of Yoga and the possibility of studying its health methods at home were what actually spurred me on in writing this book, especially after I had learned of the shocking state of the national health in the United States, where physical and mental illness statistics are ever increasing, and the number of alcoholics, narcotic addicts, delinquents and criminals is growing by leaps and bounds.

Something must have gone very wrong with us somewhere if, as official statistics indicate, one out of every three Americans (or one-third the total population) is doomed to develop cancer; if one out of every twelve children born in the United States will sooner or later become an inmate of a mental hospital; and if 52 per cent of our young men are rejected by the Army for physical or mental defects. Yet this is the general picture in the richest and most progressive country in the world. Not in India, nor in Japan, Hong Kong, Ceylon, Burma, Thailand or Cambodia (the six other Oriental countries I recently visited) did I find anything approximating this situation—in spite of all the epidemics, the unsanitary living conditions, the poverty and ignorance of hygiene.

Here at home we are successfully managing to fight infectious disease, but the number of people afflicted with degenerative disease has risen so high that, to quote from the "Report on the Health of the Nation" by Dr. W. Coda Martin, President of the American Academy of Nutrition, "This country

How Yoga Can Be of Help to You

of once strong, vigorous and adventurous people will become a nation of invalids, not only weak in body, but also weak in mind." Or to quote another doctor who had listened to that report, "We are in a mess and let's face it!"

It seems to me that, instead of trying to build rockets to reach the moon, it would be better to mobilize our resources to make sure that the number of able-bodied and mentally sound Americans shall not shrink to nothing here on earth.

Undoubtedly, there must be ways of preventing such a possible disaster if one earnestly decides to do something about it.

I feel very confident that if the study of Yoga were to be added to the curricula of our schools, colleges and training camps, it would help considerably in decreasing the menacing incidence of physical and mental disorders.

The science of Yoga has a separate division devoted to the most thorough care of the human body and all of its functions —from breathing to elimination. Its methods are entirely different from other methods of health education because Yoga aims, first of all, at removing the very causes of ill health which are brought about by insufficient oxygenation, poor nutrition, inadequate exercise and poor elimination of the waste products that poison the system. Secondly, through rhythmic breathing and concentration, as well as by influencing our glandular activity, Yoga can help to increase our mental capacities, sharpen our senses and widen our intellectual horizon. And finally, through meditation, it enables man to come closer to the realization of his own spiritual nature.

In short, Yoga can help solve the problems of any receptive individual, whether these problems be of a physical, mental, or spiritual nature and thereby, eventually, also help solve the problems of a group, society and even a nation.

The government of India, having realized the manifold advantages of Yoga, is beginning to encourage the practice of Asanas, or Yoga postures, on a nationwide scale. In Delhi, for example, Asanas are today being taught to people in all walks of life. Early in the morning open air instruction is offered in public places; special classes are even conducted for members of Parliament and foreign diplomats. The Prime Minister himself is a great Yoga enthusiast and attributes his energy and youthfulness to the daily practice of the Asanas, especially of the Headstand. He made a statement to that effect to newspaper reporters who interviewed him during his recent state visit to Japan, something which in turn prompted the Japanese publishers of my book, *Forever Young, Forever Healthy*—the first book on Yoga in Japanese, I am told—to print his picture and endorsement on the cover.

As a matter of fact even President Eisenhower, while recovering from his illness, was put on a routine of "deep breathing" exercises for ten minutes a day, according to newspaper reports. But this fact slipped by unnoticed, probably because no formal mention of Yoga was made in connection with it. A pity, as this might have started a vogue for deep breathing in America—for the public in general likes to copy the tastes and habits of their leaders and idols. Thus a great many people seem to have taken up the study of Yoga simply because Gloria Swanson, Greta Garbo, Jennifer Jones, Marilyn Monroe, Olivia de Haviland, Mala Powers, Robert Ryan, and also the world-famous beautician Elizabeth Arden, are known to have been devotees. Imagine, then, how they might be influenced by the health routine of the President of the United States!

How great an influence advocacy by a known personality can have on the public is perfectly illustrated by my own experiences in this respect. After one of my lectures in which I mentioned Gloria Swanson, for instance, I was asked more questions about her than about Yoga itself. This was all to the good, for Gloria's enthusiasm helped a great deal in making Yoga popular in this country. And when she introduced my book—and me—to the audience attending my opening lecture

How Yoga Can Be of Help to You xiii

at the Waldorf Astoria Hotel in New York, she stated unequivocally that Yoga was her health and beauty secret.

The great violinist Yehudi Menuhin considers Yoga—and sleep—to be even more important to his art than violin practice, according to an article in *Life*. His Yoga instructor in India, B. K. S. Iyengar of Poona, wears a wristwatch inscribed, "To my best violin teacher . . . from Yehudi Menuhin."

Yoga is of great value not only to artists engaged in creative work. It will help businessmen and sportsmen, public speakers, models and housewives, and also people employed in offices, factories and stores where they must either sit at a desk, stand on their feet for long hours at a time, or work under stresses and tensions. In an article entitled, "Deep Breathing Advised to Alleviate Heart Pain," Dr. George W. Crane, M.D., Ph.D., tells that the "deep breathing" technique is an excellent aid in every case of sudden heart attack, regardless of its type. "Simply lie flat, relax, breathe deeply, and let God carry on." [2]

Yoga exercises are, incidentally, an invaluable aid to keeping the figure slim and youthful, and many women will also find them effective in helping to solve their particular problems.

The six-week course outlined in these pages is arranged in such a manner that even one who has never done any exercises or has never even heard of Yoga will have no difficulty in following it.

Yoga has a very illuminating and practical message for our restless, insecure, and spiritually forlorn world of today. I earnestly hope that these lessons will be at least of some small service to those who strive for a better, healthier, and happier life. This book goes out with the blessings of my *guru* and his good wishes to all students of Yoga.

INDRA DEVI

---

[2] *Glendale News Press*, December 7, 1955.

Acknowledgments

My grateful thanks to my best friend and guide, Dr. Sigfrid Knauer, for his understanding, cooperation, and advice; and to Dr. Ehrenfried E. Pfeiffer, for the privilege of letting me use material from the manuscript of his work, *Balanced Nutrition—Know What You Eat and Why*.

I am also indebted to my friends Erica Moore, for her invaluable help in getting this manuscript into shape; Maurine Dudley Townsend, for putting finishing touches on it; and Therese Voelker for her devoted patience in copying it from my hieroglyphic handwriting.

Contents

Foreword *by Yehudi Menuhin* vii

Author's Preface: *How Yoga Can Be of Help to* You . ix

Introduction: *What You Should Know About Yoga* . . xxi

Lesson One—*First Week* 1

   What the Course Is—and How to Use It
   The Waking-Up Routine
   Deep Breathing
   Exercises for the Neck and for the Eyes
   Eye Exercises
   Yoga Postures
   Rocking
   The Raised-Legs Posture
   The Head-to-Knee Posture
   The Lotus Pose
   The Cobra Pose
   The Squatting Pose
   Breathing Exercises
   Relaxation
   General Rules and Suggestions
   Discussion on the Effects of Breathing

Lesson Two—*Second Week* 45

The Half-Headstand
Yoga Mudra (Symbol of Yoga)
The Body-Raising Pose
The Bending-Forward Posture
The Footlift Pose: First Movement
The Reverse Posture
Breathing Exercises
A Breathing Exercise for Good Posture
Rhythmic Breathing
Meditative Poses
Diet

Lesson Three—*Third Week* 85

The Headstand: First Stage
The Stretching Posture
The Plough Posture
The Camel Posture
The Lion Posture
The Footlift Pose: Second Movement
The Cleansing Breath
The Walking Breathing Exercise
On Relaxation and the Endocrine Glands

Lesson Four—*Fourth Week* 111

The Headstand: Second Stage
The Swan Posture
The Twist Posture: First Movement
The Abdominal Lift
The Churning Pose
The Footlift Pose: Third Movement
Breathing Exercises
On the Kundalini Power

CONTENTS   xix

Lesson Five—*Fifth Week* **137**

The Headstand: Third Stage
The Triangle Pose
The Twist Posture: Second Movement
The Shoulderstand
The Supine Pose
Breathing Exercises
The Recharging Breath
The Wood-Chopping Movement
On the Yama-Niyama and Contemplation

Lesson Six—*Sixth Week* **159**

Practice Schedule
The Angular Rest Pose
The Angular Balance Pose
The Twist Posture: Third Movement
Breathing Exercises
The Mountain Pose
Second Breathing Exercise
On Concentration and Meditation

Appendix I: *Discussion of Diet and Recipes* . . . **181**

The Hay Diet Food Classification
Cleansing Diet
Health Diet
Reducing Diet
Diet for People Over Thirty-five
Recipes

Appendix II: *Letters to the Author* **197**

Index **215**

Introduction

WHAT YOU SHOULD KNOW ABOUT YOGA

WELCOME, FRIEND, TO THE EVER-GROWING CIRCLE OF YOGA students here in the Americas as well as the world over. Let us hope that the study and practice of this most ancient, yet still unsurpassed, art and science of living will give you the key to youth, health and long life, and help you find harmony, peace of mind and true happiness. It has done that for countless people throughout the centuries, and it is now your turn to try this age-old method and test its effectiveness. For, unless you yourself are benefited by Yoga, no recounting of even the most wonderful results achieved by others will be of the slightest use to you.

Once you have started the Yoga practices, their influence will soon become apparent in your everyday life. You will begin to enjoy better health, sounder sleep, a keener mind and a more cheerful disposition. Your body will gradually acquire a pleasant lightness and suppleness, your mind will become more calm and your tensions diminish. You will also notice an improvement in your figure, posture, vision, and general appearance, for you will start looking younger and feeling more alive.

The secret of Yoga lies in the fact that it deals with the

entire man, not with just one of his aspects. It is concerned with growth—physical, mental, moral and spiritual. It develops forces that are already within you. Beginning with improved health and added physical well-being, it works up slowly through the mental to the spiritual. The transition is so gradual that you may not even be aware of it until you realize that a change in you has already taken place.

The following passage from a writing on Yoga will explain how this actually happens:

> When a student of Yoga determines and rightly directs his course, a molecular change takes place in his body until, in about six months, this change begins to affect his tastes and habits. It also expands the power of his mind. As the force within him becomes awakened, his state of consciousness also changes—he ceases to be lonely, his fears vanish and his happiness comes within his reach.

The advanced stages of Yoga require many years of special preparation—practices for which the American mode of living, its tempo and surroundings, are not well suited. Under existing circumstances these advanced practices may even prove dangerous and detrimental to your physical and mental well-being and balance. It is better, therefore, to leave them alone and to limit yourself to the practice of the Yoga postures and deep breathing and relaxation exercises, with some of the time devoted to concentration and meditation.

Before we begin the important part of our first lesson, the deep breathing and postures, I would like to give you, in question-and-answer form, a general idea of Yoga so that you, as a student, may know some facts about it. But first, please do not make the mistake so common in America of using the words *Yogi* and *Yoga* interchangeably. *Yoga* is a science that gives a human being the knowledge of his true Self, whereas a *yogi* is a man who has mastered this science; he may also be called a *yógin,* while a woman is a *yógini.*

What You Should Know About Yoga

Many people still think that Yoga is a religion. Others believe it to be a kind of magic. Some associate Yoga with the rope trick, with snake-charming, fire-eating or sitting on nail-beds, lying on broken glass, walking on sharp swords, etc. Sometimes it is even linked to fortune telling, spiritualism, hypnotism and other "isms." In reality, *Yoga is a method, a system of physical, mental and spiritual development.*

Q: What is the meaning of the word "Yoga"?

A: The word *Yoga* is derived from the Sanskrit root "yuj," which means join, or union. The purpose of all Yogas is to unite man, the finite, with the Infinite, with Cosmic Consciousness, Truth, God, Light or whatever other name one chooses to call the Ultimate Reality. Yoga, as they say in India, is a marriage of spirit and matter.

Q: Is there only one Yoga?

A: Yoga has several branches or divisions, but the goal, the aim of all of them is the same—the achievement of a union with the Supreme Consciousness. In *Karma Yoga,* for instance, this is achieved through work and action; in *Jnana (or Gnani) Yoga,* through knowledge and study; in *Bhakti Yoga,* through devotion and selfless love; in *Mantra Yoga* through repetitions of certain invocations and sounds. *Raja Yoga* (Royal Yoga) is the Yoga of consciousness, the highest form of Yoga. Its practice usually starts with *Hatha Yoga* which gives the body the necessary health and strength to endure the hardships of the more advanced stages of training.

Hatha Yoga is the Yoga of physical well-being. It consists of several steps and is preceded by the *Yama-Niyama,* the ten rules of the Yoga code of morality. The first stage is called *Asana,* or posture; the second is *Pranayama,* or breath control; the third is *Pratyahara* or nerve control; the fourth is *Dharana,* or mind control; the fifth is *Dhyiana,* or meditation; and finally there is *Samadhi,* the state of ultimate bliss and spiritual enlightenment. Strictly speaking the last four stages of Hatha Yoga already merge into the realm of Raja Yoga.

Q: What does "Hatha" mean?

A: Ha stands for the sun and *tha* for the moon. The correct translation of *Hatha Yoga* would be solar and lunar Yoga, since it deals with the solar and lunar qualities of breath and Prana.

Q: What is "Prana"?

A: Prana is a subtle life energy existing in the air in fluid form. Everything living, from men to amoebae, from plants to animals, is charged with Prana. Without Prana there is no life.

Q: What religion does a yogi profess?

A: A yogi can belong to any religion or to none at all. In this case, he usually forms his own relationship with the Ultimate Reality once he has come closer to It.

Q: Can a Catholic take up Yoga?

A: Certainly, since Yoga is not a religion. In fact, a Catholic association has been recently formed in Bangalore, India, in order to introduce the Yoga Asanas to the Catholic young men there, and to integrate them into the Catholic way of life.

Q: If the goal of Yoga is a spiritual illumination, why then is so much attention given to the care of the body?

A: The yogis regard the human body as a temple of the Living Spirit and believe that as such it should be brought to the highest state of perfection. Also, the advanced practices of Yoga require great power of endurance. The body might not be able to stand the strain without special preparation.

Q: What is the origin of Yoga?

A: Yoga was originated in India several thousand years ago. According to the German Professor Max Mueller, Yoga is about 6,000 years old, but other sources suggest it is much older than that.

Q: Who originated Yoga?

What You Should Know About Yoga

A: This is not known. Patanjali, who lived about 200 B.C., is called the Father of Yoga because he was the first to put into writing what had until that time been handed down only verbally from master, or *guru*, to pupil, or *chela*.

Q: Can the average American take up Yoga for the improvement of his physical condition?

A: The Yoga postures, breathing and relaxation exercises can be taken up by anyone who wants to improve his physical or mental condition. One need not go into the more advanced stages of the training.

Q: What is the age limit for a Yoga student?

A: Normally, one should not start before the age of six and not after the age of sixty-five, although many people do start later and still obtain good results—see the letter on page 204 in Appendix II. One can continue the practice of Yoga postures for the rest of one's life.

Q: Can Yoga cure disease?

A: Yoga cannot cure anything. The healing work is done by nature. Yoga exercises can only help remove impurities and obstructions, so that nature may be given a chance to accomplish her task successfully.

Q: What is the difference between Yoga exercises and other gymnastics?

A: Yoga Asanas are an art applied to the anatomy of the living body, whereas gymnastics are a form of engineering applied to the muscles of the body. The aim of Yoga postures is not merely the superficial development of muscles. These postures tend to normalize the functions of the entire organism, to regulate the involuntary processes of respiration, circulation, digestion, elimination, metabolism, etc., and to affect the working of all the glands and organs, as well as the nervous system and the mind. This result is achieved by doing deep breathing while the body is placed in various postures. Each of these exercises creates a different totality in the functional relationship within the organism. Hence, Yoga is able to influence man physically, mentally, morally and spiritually. Yoga emphasizes the philosophy of exercise. Under its training one experiences a sense of awakening. All of one's capacities are heightened, and one achieves balance and stamina through these exercises, some of which are modelled after the movements of various animals. In Yoga, relaxation is taught as an art, breathing as a science, and mental control of the body as a means of harmonizing the body, mind, and spirit.

Infinite energy is at the disposal of man if he knows how to get it, and this is a part of the science of Yoga.

ADAMS BECK, *The Story of Philosophy*

Lesson One

FIRST WEEK

Only a few men die from sudden lack of air, but multitudes perish because for years they have not been breathing enough.
—RASMUS ALSAKER, M.D., *Master Key Is Health*

WHAT THE COURSE IS—AND HOW TO USE IT

As the title of my book implies, the course of exercises outlined here for home practice is designed to teach the rudiments of Yoga so that they can be incorporated into the daily routine of the average man or woman living in our Western world. I have taken into account not only the pace to which life in the United States is geared, but also the fact that most of you have not had a chance to keep your muscles limber and your joints supple. At first glance, as you look through the illustrations in the book, some of the Yoga poses may seem impossibly difficult to you—you may feel you cannot even attempt them. But please do not be frightened away. If you follow instructions, with a little patience and method you will be able to learn a great deal more than you think possible—in less time than you imagine.

The course is divided into six lessons. Each lesson consists of a number of breathing exercises and Yoga postures—probably more than you will normally have time for. You will find yourself liking some better than others, and you may as well let personal preference guide you when it comes to choosing those you want to incorporate into your own personal routine. Once having decided, repeat your chosen routine every day for a week, in order to give yourself a chance to assimilate it before going on to the next week's set of instructions. As you practice the same postures day by day, you will find your muscles stretching, your body growing more responsive and better controlled, until what seemed unattainable on Monday has become routine on Saturday. Then you will be ready to go on to the next week's lesson.

I also want to make clear that throughout the book I have tried, in outlining each day's schedule, to approximate the normal waking and sleeping hours of the average person. Those who keep odd bed and meal hours will need to adjust this schedule, making whatever changes are necessary in order to suit their particular time requirements. The best time is, of course, in the morning before breakfast, but it does not matter too much at what time of day the exercises are done, just so long as they are done on an empty stomach. Allow three to four hours after a big meal, one and one-half to two hours after a light meal, and about half an hour after a glass of juice. It is also inadvisable to do the exercises directly before eating. *But the most important thing is to do them regularly, without skipping.* If you happen not to have time for all of them, do just a few, perhaps even only one when you are in a great hurry—but never omit them entirely. Once you begin to skip, you are likely to do so more and more often until you stop exercising altogether.

First Week

THE WAKING-UP ROUTINE

We shall begin our first lesson with the routine you should adopt the moment you have opened your eyes in the morning and are ready to get up.

First of all, learn to wake up properly. Do some stretching. Stretch your arms, yawn several times, stretch your legs, stretch your whole body. While you are still in bed, do the following stretching exercise:

Keeping your feet together, toe to toe, start to push out the right leg, without raising it off the mattress, as if wanting to lengthen it. The pull will be felt from the hip down and the leg will be momentarily lengthened by an inch or more. Hold your leg in this position while you count to sixty, then relax, allowing the right foot to become even again with the left one. Repeat with the left leg.

This exercise stretches the spinal column and tones up the sympathetic nerves. It has a rejuvenating effect on the entire body. As this is a very potent nerve exercise, you must be careful not to overdo it. Sixty seconds for each leg is the maximum. You may, however, repeat the exercise again in the evening, if you wish. If your mattress is too soft, don't do this in bed, but wait until you are ready to do the other exercises on the floor and simply begin with this one.

Incidentally, if you want to avoid those "morning backaches" or a tired feeling in your back, don't ever sleep on a soft mattress. Get a hard one or put a board under the soft one. Just try it out for a week or so and you will notice the difference in the way you feel. I myself, when traveling or staying in hotels, often pull the mattress down to the floor, unless it is too heavy. If I find I cannot handle the mattress, I slip the glass top from a dressing table under it.

Another important thing to bear in mind is never to *jump*

out of bed, even if you are in a hurry, as this gives the whole nervous system a shock. Give yourself a little time to return to this world from the threshold of another. Make this transition slowly and gradually and give your body time to "shift gears." Animals offer a good example of natural behavior. Watch a dog or a cat, for instance. Except when in danger or emergency, they never jump up, but keep yawning and stretching for quite a while after coming awake; then they slowly get up on their feet. Imitate them. When you finally get out of bed, drink a glass of water, but water that is at room temperature, not iced. Drink it after brushing your teeth and cleaning your tongue with a special tongue scraper or with a wash cloth. The tongue, as you probably know, is a barometer that shows the condition of your intestinal tract. A bright red tongue indicates a clean intestinal tract, whereas a coated tongue indicates the opposite. If the latter is the case, you had better plan to go on a cleansing diet or fast for a few days to get rid of the impurities accumulated in your body. We shall discuss this at length later on.

Now let us return to the exercises. As has already been said, they should be done with an empty stomach, empty bladder and also, if possible, empty bowels. When you are ready to start, put on a minimum of clothing and make sure that whatever you are wearing is comfortable and not tight. Do not wear a girdle, bra, tight belt or the like while exercising. You may wear a pair of socks if your feet feel too cold.

DEEP BREATHING

Yoga emphasizes our relationship to the universe and therefore teaches a breathing different from the usual breathing, a breathing that reflects our inner attitude while we are performing it. This attitude is one of devotion toward the com-

First Week

munion with the All, and should be maintained all the time one is doing deep breathing.

Conscious Breathing

I shall begin with an explanation of Yoga breathing, as it is most important for you first of all to understand how this deep breathing is done and how it differs from ordinary breathing.

Usually we are not conscious of our breathing. Breath passes through our bodies like dream waves. In Yoga, this process is lifted to the level of consciousness. It is you, yourself, who take over the direction and control of the air-flow.

In normal respiration the air is taken in through the nostrils without any special effort, sound or exaggerated movement of the nose or chest. In short, it is done unconsciously. We are not even aware of air traveling through our nostrils, down the nasal and oral parts of the pharynx, of its reaching the larynx and then the trachea and the lungs. More than that, not only are we unaware of the breathing process, but most of us don't know anything about it. You can easily prove this for yourself by asking several friends to answer this simple question: "What happens to the air after it enters the nostrils?" They will probably tell you that it goes to the lungs, although everybody realizes in a general way that the nose does not reach that far in and that there is quite a distance between it and the lungs.

Taking into consideration the limited knowledge we possess about the function of our organism, I will try to make the anatomical explanations as simple as possible. It is very easy to demonstrate the deep-breathing technique, but not nearly so easy to put it in words. We shall therefore go into it in some detail so that you may be able to grasp the idea correctly.

The Anatomy of Breathing

Let us begin by analyzing the way the so-called Yoga deep-breathing exercise is usually done and see in what way it differs from ordinary deep breathing.

Take a deep breath. Just put down the book for a moment and do it the way you have always been doing it. Most people vigorously sniff air in through the nostrils, simultaneously raising the chest and popping out the eyes. Yoga deep breathing is not done this way at all. Let us examine what happens when you take the usual kind of deep breath. First of all you interrupt your normal—or unconscious—breathing and make a conscious, deliberate effort to inhale. In doing this, you use considerable force. You also produce a loud sniffing sound by automatically contracting the nostrils. In Yoga deep breathing the process is so entirely different that it is better to completely forget the way you have been doing it and learn anew. To begin with, *you do not consciously use the nostrils at all;* they remain completely inactive during inhalation and exhalation. Instead, you draw in the air by using the area situated at the back wall of your mouth, called the pharyngeal area. This connects the mouth with the nose, and is the continuation of the nasal openings which end behind the soft palate leading from the mouth into the throat.

You will understand this still better if you will take a hand mirror and look into it, opening your mouth wide. (I suggest that you once again interrupt your reading and pick up a mirror right now, otherwise you may forget about it.) What you see, especially if you press down the tongue, is a wall in the form of a dome. The air passage is located directly under this dome. This is the pharyngeal area. And it is this area instead of the nostrils which you must learn to use in Yoga deep breathing. This, then, is the main technical difference between ordinary deep breathing and Yoga deep breathing.

First Week

Have you ever before been aware of the possibility of drawing in a breath through an area other than the nostrils? Probably not. However, people suffering from a post-nasal drip are made very conscious of this other area.

If you sniff in water, especially salt water, through the nostrils and eject it through the mouth, you will instantly become aware of the pharyngeal area, which connects the mouth with the nose. It is this connection that makes it possible to draw the air in through the pharyngeal area, while keeping the nostrils completely inactive during deep breathing. The action is felt *only* at the back of the throat during the exhalaation and the impression is that of a hydraulic suction pump or press operating in the back of the mouth. In fact, the entire action is similar, since during inhalation one feels as if the air were being drawn in, and during exhalation as if it were being pressed down the throat, though in reality, of course, it is being expelled.

It really should not be too difficult for you to do the deep-breathing routine since you have already been doing it for a long time, and without any instructions. Without your being aware of it, this is what takes place while you sleep, for in sleep the sense organism is not functioning and cannot therefore interfere with the rhythm of breathing. When asleep we automatically, or shall I say instinctively, resort to deep breathing at certain intervals. This probably is an indication that deep breathing is of an elemental nature and we can, by means of it, consciously establish a contact between our inner selves and the deep forces of Nature.

Learning to Breathe Correctly

Since you know how to do deep breathing while asleep, a simple method of learning to do it during wakefulness should be to simulate sleep. Lie down, close your eyes, relax the whole body, drop the chin and imagine that you are asleep, thus letting your breathing become deeper and deeper. But first a word of warning: When exaggerated and overstrained, deep breathing leads to snoring, so you had better learn to relax and breathe softly and gently! Also, the next time you happen to be in a room with someone who is fast asleep, listen for a while to his or her respiration; you will quickly notice the difference, both in sound and rhythm, between the "waking" and the "sleeping" breath.

In Yoga deep breathing, you start filling the lower part of the lungs first, then you fill the middle and upper part. When exhaling you first empty the upper part of the lungs, then the middle, and last of all the lower part.

This process, however, is not divided into three separate actions. Inhalation is done in one smooth continuous flow just as one might pour water in filling a glass. First the bottom is filled, then the middle, and finally the upper portion. But the process itself—pouring in order to fill the entire glass—is an uninterrupted one. Just so is the air taken in, in one uninterrupted inhalation, while the lungs fill with air; just so is the air expelled until the lungs are empty. *But you must do it slowly and in a most relaxed manner. No effort or strain should ever be exerted. This is very important.*

You then become aware of the function of your own diaphragm. You expand the flanks when inhaling and contract them when exhaling. The lower part of the rib cage naturally expands first when you breathe in and is compressed last when you let the air out. This too should be done gently, *without any force or strain. The chest remains motionless and passive* during the entire process of respiration. *Only* the ribs expand during inhalation and contract during exhalation, accordion-fashion. *To use force during inhalation is completely wrong.* One should do it with ease, without any tension or strain whatever. In deep breathing, exhalation is as important as inhalation because it eliminates poisonous matter. The lower part of our lungs seldom are sufficiently emptied, and tend to accumulate air saturated with waste products, for with ordinary breathing we never expel enough of the carbon dioxide our system throws off even if we do inhale enough oxygen. If, on the other hand, the lower part of the lungs are properly expanded and contracted, the circulation in the liver and spleen, which are thus "massaged" by the diaphragm, are greatly benefited.

Another important thing to remember is that while doing deep breathing *the spine should be kept straight,* so as not to impair the free flow of the life-force, or *Prana.* This also helps to develop correct posture. The yogis attach such great importance to correct posture that they have devised several different positions for their various advanced breathing practices as well as for meditation and concentration.

The favorite posture is the Lotus Pose, or *Padmāsana,* a word derived from *Padma,* which means lotus in Sanskrit, and *Asana,* which means posture. (The accent in Padmāsana falls on the first syllable of the second word, Asana, not on the second as would be natural in English.) The other three postures are *Siddhāsana, Swastikāsana,* and *Samāsana.* You will learn them one by one later on.

In all of these postures the spine has to be kept erect, in one straight line with the head, neck and trunk. The necessity for keeping the spine straight is emphasized in all Yoga practices where it is a must. We human beings are the only inhabitants of this planet who have a vertical spine, whereas in animals it extends horizontally. Only man, the crowning creation, through the awakening of his consciousness has acquired a vertical spine. Yoga reminds us of this; it is considered a symbolical connecting link between earth and heaven.

When you sit down on the floor with your legs crossed, visualize a stream running through you in a straight line, starting at the top of your head and continuing into the ground.

Imagine, too, that this is the axis around which your body has been moulded. This will help you learn to sit up straight without being stiff and tense. You should, in fact, feel comfortable and relaxed as you sit this way.

Your First Deep Breath

Now as you sit down on your exercise mat, get ready to start your first real lesson in deep breathing. If for some reason you are unable to sit on the floor, you may sit on a chair or else stand up. Deep breathing can also be done lying down, provided the spine is kept straight. But normally we should do it while sitting cross-legged. If you cannot assume the Lotus Pose as yet, cross your legs in any way easiest for you. (The complete technique for assuming the Lotus Pose is given later in this lesson.)

Again, first check your posture. The spine should be straight, the head erect, hands on knees, eyes closed. Now concentrate on the pharyngeal space at the back wall of your mouth and, slightly contracting its muscles, begin to draw in the air through that space as if you were using a suction pump. Do it slowly and steadily, letting the pumping sound be clearly heard. Don't use the nostrils; remember that they remain inactive during the entire respiration process. When inhaling let your ribs expand sideways like an accordion—beginning with the lower ones, of course. Remember the chest and shoulders should remain motionless. The entire inhalation should be done gently and effortlessly. When it has been completed pause for a second or two, holding the breath. Then slowly begin breathing out. The exhalation is usually not as passive as the inhalation. You use a slight, a very slight, pressure to push the air out—although it feels as though you pressed it against the throat like a hydraulic press. The upper ribs are now contracted first, the nostrils remain inactive and the chest

First Week

and shoulders motionless. At the end of the exhalation, pull in the stomach a little so as to push out all the air.

You have just taken your first deep breath.

The beginner should not try to take too full a breath at once. Start by breathing to the count of four. Then hold the breath, counting to two, and start slowly exhaling, again to the count of four. Breathing in and out to an equal number of beats is called rhythmic breathing. You allow four beats to fill your lungs, two to retain the breath, and four to breathe out. The respiration should be timed in such a way that at the end of the four beats you have *completed the exhalation*. Don't just stop at the end of the count when there is still air to be expelled. You should adjust your breathing to the timing. Repeat, but do not take more than 5 or 6 deep breaths at one time during the first week. This is enough for today. You shouldn't do more even if you are enjoying it. Be careful not to overdo the breathing, especially inhalation, as this may lead to unpleasant results such as dizziness, nausea, headaches, even fainting spells due to hyperventilation caused by a sudden, excessive intake of oxygen. You should not invite unnecessary trouble instead of getting full benefit out of these lessons. As your teacher, it is my duty to warn you against possible ill effects caused by over-breathing. Please be patient; it is for your own good that I am offering this advice.

Deep breathing is often quite a revelation to people who do it for the first time. "I just discovered my lungs," a man once said to me. Incidentally he happened to be a photographer who came with a reporter to take my picture during an interview. Both got interested in Yoga and admitted they badly needed it because, to use their own words, "everybody in the newspaper office has an ulcer and suffers from tension."

If you want to see how the ribs expand during inhalation

and contract during exhalation, watch yourself in the mirror. The chest should then remain uncovered, of course, at least to the waistline. It should also be a joy to you to "discover your lungs," and to know that you can consciously take a deep breath and direct it to any part of your body you desire.

EXERCISES FOR THE NECK AND FOR THE EYES

Now we are going to take up the exercises for the neck and for the eyes which will help do away with eye strain, tension, and stiffness of the neck. You can do them whenever you please—at the beginning of the lesson, at the end of it, or at any other convenient time.

A number of my students practice these exercises while taking a bath, listening to the radio, or at intervals while at work, whether at a typewriter or a kitchen sink. One of my friends does them in the car while waiting for his wife to finish shopping; another while the commercials are on, when he watches T.V. It all depends how much time one has to spare.

Before starting these exercises, see for yourself how flexible your neck is; then decide whether or not it needs to be exercised.

Just drop your head forward, then rotate it several times. If the rolling goes smoothly without any grinding or crackling noises you have nothing to worry about; if it doesn't, better try the neck exercises.

Usually the trouble begins when the joints, or rather their linings, are inadequately lubricated and begin to stiffen from accumulation of calcium deposits—a sign of old age regardless of how many or how few years ago you were born. As one new student remarked after finishing the exercises, "It sounds as if I were eating gravel!" This crunching sound is certainly a warning of impending trouble—unnecessary trouble, too, as one can preserve one's elasticity, health, and youthful appearance by

First Week

spending a few minutes a day doing the right type of exercise.

TECHNIQUE: Here is how the neck exercises are to be done:

Sit on the floor with your legs crossed and keep the hands on the knees. If you prefer to sit on a chair, choose a hard one, otherwise you will find it difficult to keep your *back straight,* which is essential.

Relax the whole body. You should be conscious of it only from the neck up—the rest should remain motionless and as unstrained as if you were sitting under water up to the neck.

1. Now close your eyes and effortlessly and gently let your head drop forward and backward, then again forward and backward. Do each exercise four times to begin with. Later on you can increase the number to six or more. When dropping the head backward keep your facial muscles relaxed; the lips should part slightly when the head is thrown back.

2. In the next exercise, you first turn your head to the extreme right and return it to normal position; then turn to the extreme left and return to normal again. Repeat four times. Turning the head to the sides contracts the muscles, returning to normal position relaxes them.

3. In the third exercise you bend your head to the right as if someone were pulling your right ear towards the right shoulder, and straighten the head, bend it to the left and straighten again. Repeat four times.

When bending the head to the side, *don't lift the shoulder,* and don't tilt the head either—let it move only from its upright position into an almost horizontal one, otherwise there will be very little pull in the neck. This pull should be strongly felt in the left side of the neck when the head is bent to the right; in the right side when the head is bent to the left.

4. The next exercise resembles the neck movements of a turtle, for you should literally "stick your neck out" as far as you can, then draw it back again. In doing so, you will make a gliding movement forward with your chin, as if trying to

reach far out with it and thus to lengthen the neck. Here the pull will be felt in the back of the neck on both sides between the ears as well as in the middle. Repeat this exercise four times.

5. In the last exercise, do the same movement that you did to test the elasticity of your neck. Drop your head forward and feel it grow lifeless and heavy, then let it slowly roll clockwise several times; repeat counterclockwise the same number of times. Do not stiffen the back or shoulders, but let the head hang relaxed so it will roll like that of a sleeping baby or someone who has had too many drinks.

At the end of the last exercise, pat the neck with the back of both hands, smacking it under the chin and on the sides. To pat the back of the neck, use your palms and finger tips.

The daily practice of these exercises will loosen up the tension in your neck muscles and keep them relaxed and elastic. It will also control any tendency to a double chin and help to improve your eyesight. The vision gets better and clearer as the ophthalmic, or eye, nerves receive a richer supply of blood.

EYE EXERCISES

Remain sitting in the same position as before. Open your eyes, then check on your posture. Is your spine erect? Hands on the knees? Body relaxed? Head straight? That is how you should always remain while doing eye exercises. The whole body must be motionless; nothing must move except the eyes.

Now raise your eyes and find a small point that you can see clearly without straining, without frowning, without becoming tense and, of course, without moving your head. While doing this exercise look at this point each time you raise your eyes.

Next, lower your eyes to find a small point on the floor which you can see clearly when glancing down. Look at it each time

First Week

you lower your eyes. Breathing should be normal—that is, you don't have to do deep breathing.

TECHNIQUE:

1. (a) Raise the eyes to look at your chosen high point.
   (b) Lower the eyes to look at your chosen low point.
   Repeat four times. Close the eyes and rest a moment.

2. Now do the same using points to your right and to your left, at eye level. Keep your raised fingers or two pencils on each side as guides and adjust them so that you can see them clearly when moving the eyes to the right and to the left, but without straining.

   Keeping the fingers at eye level, and moving only the eyes, look to the right at your chosen point, then to the left. Repeat four times. Blink several times, then close your eyes and rest.

3. Next choose a point you can see from the right corner of your eyes when you raise them, and another that you can see from the left corner of your eyes when you lower them, half closing the lids. Remember to retain your original posture—spine erect, hands on knees, head straight and motionless.

   Look at your chosen point in right corner up, then to the one in left corner down. Repeat four times. Blink several times. Close the eyes and rest.

   Now do the same exercise in reverse. That is, first look to the left corner up, then to the right corner down. Repeat four times. Blink several times. Close the eyes and rest.

4. Next is an exercise which should not be done until three or four days after you have begun the course. It consists of slowly rolling the eyes first clockwise, then counterclockwise as follows: Lower your eyes and look at the floor, then slowly move the eyes to the left, higher and higher until you see the ceiling. Now continue circling to the right, lower and lower down, until you see the floor again. Do this slowly, making a full-vision circle. Blink, close your eyes and rest. Then repeat the same action counterclockwise.

5. Next comes a changing-vision exercise. While doing it you alternately shift your vision from close to distant points several times.

Take a pencil, or use your finger, and hold it under the tip of your nose. Then start moving it away, without raising it, until you have fixed it at the closest possible distance where you can see it clearly without any blur. Then raise your eyes a little, look straight into the distance and there find a small point which you can also see very clearly.

Now look at the closer point—the pencil or your finger tip—then shift to the farther point in the distance. Repeat several times, blink, close your eyes and squeeze them tight.

6. And now for the palming which is most important for preserving the eyesight. Palming also has a beneficial, relaxing effect on your nervous system.

Remain seated on the floor. Draw up your knees, keeping your feet on the floor and slightly apart. Now briskly rub your palms to charge them with electricity and place the cupped palms over your closed eyes. The fingers of the right hand should be crossed over the fingers of the left hand on the forehead. The elbows should rest on your raised knees and the neck should be kept straight. Don't bend your head. Do the deep breathing while palming your eyes.

If you are going to do the palming for longer than a few minutes, better sit down at a table, place some books or pillows in front of you to support your elbows so that you will be able to keep the neck straight, and palm the eyes in this position. I know of a man who did this for two hours at a stretch every day in order to regain his lost vision. But bear in mind that during a long session like this deep breathing can be done only now and then at long intervals. If the palming is done for only a short period, however, one can do deep breathing for half a minute or so at first, gradually increasing it every week.

First Week

YOGA POSTURES

> *Of all creatures, the human being has the least sense for management of his body.*
>
> —EHRENFRIED E. PFEIFFER, M.D. PH.D.

You are now ready to start learning the Yoga postures. Naturally we shall begin with the simplest ones, then as your joints and muscles start to limber up we shall proceed to those that are more difficult to do. Please do not allow yourself to be frightened away or easily discouraged. Remember that these are not calisthenics, that you are not in competition with yourself or anyone else, and that none of the exercises must be forced. Be satisfied to make progress slowly. You will be amazed to discover how much your body will soon be able to do.

Rocking

Let us begin with the bracing Rocking exercise. This exercise helps overcome the drowsiness and stiffness that one so often feels on waking in the morning. As you do the Rocking exercise, you will also experience an agreeable, invigorating sensation due to the fact that your vertebrae are being given a good massage. This exercise will limber up your spine and keep it in a flexible and youthful condition. The yogis say that you can dodge old age as long as your spine remains elastic and strong. Rocking will also help you to sleep better and more soundly. I remember the effect it had on one of my students, an officer in the British army, who had been suffering from insomnia. About a week after he started studying with me, he burst into the class triumphantly announcing that he had slept the night through without any pills. He has probably slept like a baby ever since.

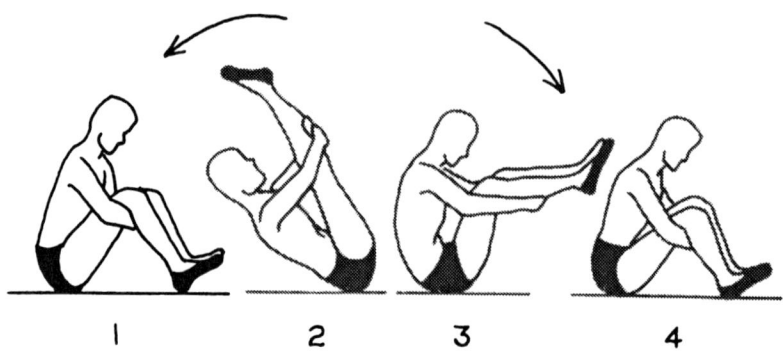

The Rocking exercise, for keeping the spine flexible and youthful.

Rocking is actually a very simple exercise, and in a few days you will be able to do it without difficulty regardless of your age, stiffness, and even weight.

TECHNIQUE: Sit down at the end of the exercise pad to make sure that your back will not hit the hard floor. Draw up your knees, and bend your head down. Put your hands under your knees. You can join your hands or not, whichever is easiest in the beginning. Now, keeping your spine rounded, swing back and forth, back and forth, in quick successive movements imitating the swinging motions of a rocking chair. Don't straighten your spine as you rock backward or you will find yourself lying flat on your back, unable to swing forward again. Don't try to do the rocking movement too slowly either, at least not in the beginning. Just imagine you are a rocking chair in motion, and enjoy the fun of it.

Here is another helpful hint: Straighten the knees just as you swing backward and then immediately bend them again as you swing forward. Don't pause after you have swung back but simply continue the to-and-fro movement. Otherwise you may get "stuck."

First Week 19

You may feel a little clumsy and awkward the first day, or you may even be afraid of losing your balance and falling down. This can hardly happen, remember, since you are already down on the floor. In a few days, when you grow accustomed to rocking, you will probably enjoy this exercise as much as I do, and you will appreciate its bracing and invigorating effects. Again, remember to keep the spine rounded and the head bent forward all the time, otherwise you will bump it against the floor when you swing backward—and never again want to do this exercise, which otherwise may well become your favorite.

On the second or third day, you can try to combine rocking with deep breathing. Inhale while rocking backwards and exhale while returning forward. Be sure not to have any zippers, buttons, hooks or buckles in the way when rocking backward or you may be in for an unpleasant and even painful sensation.

TIME: Do this exercise four to six times, then lie down to relax until your breath returns to normal again; finally take a few deep breaths while still lying on the floor.

BENEFITS: The Rocking exercise stimulates the flow of nervous energy through the spinal cord and establishes a better connection between the central nervous system and the rest of the body.

Raised-Legs Posture

Your next exercise will be the Raised-Legs Posture, *Udhitta Padāsana* in Sanskrit. Its technique is not difficult to grasp, but it may take a little time before you are able to execute it properly.

TECHNIQUE: Lie down on your back, hands along your sides. Inhale a deep breath while raising the right leg until it is at right angles to your body. Stay in this position for a while, without bending the knee, keeping the other leg flat on the floor. Then start exhaling while slowly lowering the leg again.

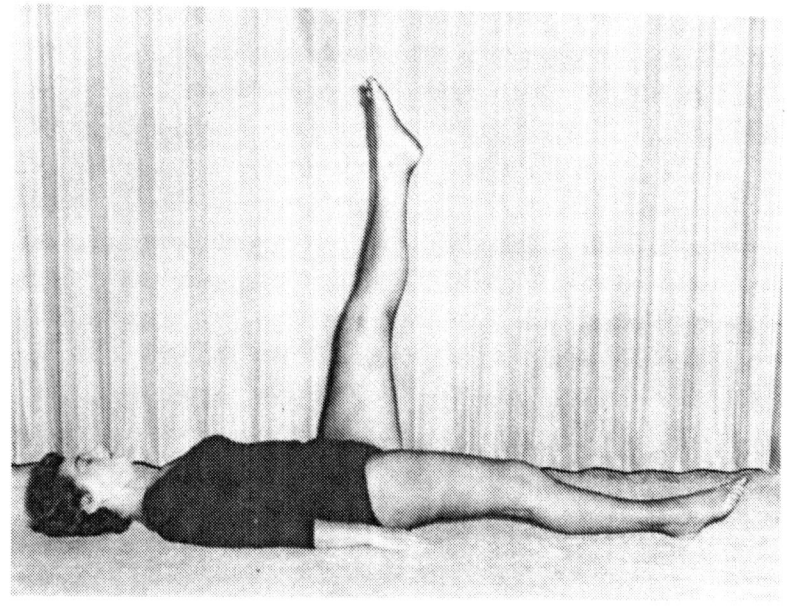

Raised-legs Posture, or *Udhitta Padāsana*, for strengthening and reducing a flabby abdomen. (Photo by Jim Buhr)

Repeat with the left leg, then with both legs at once. Now take a rest.

TIME: Hold this position three seconds, gradually increasing it to twelve seconds. At the start do the exercise only once or twice. After a few days you can try raising and lowering both legs together four or five times without stopping.

BENEFITS: This posture gives the abdomen an internal vibrating massage, thereby strengthening the muscles and reducing the fat. It is a good exercise for people who have a flabby abdomen.

You may find it difficult in the beginning to lower both legs slowly especially as they come closer to the floor. However, you will improve before the week is over. Your abdominal muscles will probably feel a little sore the day after you start, as this

First Week 21

exercise gives them a strong massage. But this will be only temporary.

CAUTION: This posture should not be done by women suffering from female disorders or by anyone who has a weak heart.

Head-to-Knee Posture

Next we shall do the Head-to-Knee Posture, called *Janushirshāsana* in Sanskrit—from *Janu* meaning knee, *Shirsh* meaning head, and *Asana* meaning posture.

TECHNIQUE: Sit up *straight* with both legs stretched out. Then bend the left knee and place the sole of the left foot against the right thigh, as high as possible.

Inhale deeply, slightly raise the upper part of the body to draw in the stomach, then exhale slowly, while bending forward to get hold of your right foot with both hands. The forehead should touch the right knee. Release the posture.

TIME: Remain in this posture for three seconds, gradually increasing the time to ten seconds. Repeat once or twice, then reverse legs and bend the head toward the left knee. After this lie down and relax. Take a few deep breaths before sitting up again. When you reach the point where you are able to keep this posture for a longer period than you can hold your breath, simply resume breathing while remaining in this position.

BENEFITS: The Head-to-Knee Posture is a helpful exercise in more than one way. It is good for preventing or relieving indigestion, constipation, and troubles arising from an enlarged spleen. It tones up sluggish bowels, strengthens the legs and adds to your energy and vitality.

In the beginning you will probably find it difficult to reach your outstretched foot with your hands. You may even begin to wonder whether your arms are not too short. The fault, however, is usually not with the arms, but with the abdomen which has grown too large or with the spine which has lost

LESSON ONE

Preparation: Bend the left knee, placing left foot against right thigh, as high as possible. (Photo by Jim Buhr)

Bend forward, holding right foot with both hands. Touch forehead to right knee. (Photo by David Hernandez)

The use of a strap or belt will make the early days of practice easier. (Photo by Jim Buhr)

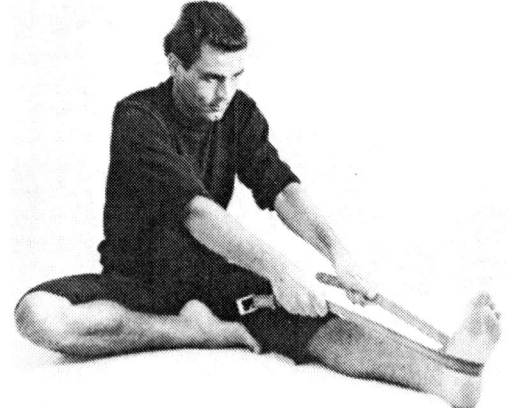

The Head-to-Knee Posture, or *Janushirshāsana*

First Week

its flexibility. The moment you limber up, you will find no difficulty in reaching your feet.

Meanwhile, simply get hold of your calves, ankles, or toes and grasp them firmly while bending the head toward the knee, even if it does take some time before you are actually able to reach the knee with your forehead. Lack of immediate success need not discourage you. I too had the same difficulty when I first started, nor did I believe I would ever be able to accomplish this feat. The important thing if you want to get results is to keep practicing daily.

You may find it easier to do this exercise with the aid of a strap or belt as shown in the picture on page 22. As you bend forward, shorten the strap, letting your hands come closer and closer to the end of the loop. You will be surprised to find that in a comparatively short time you will be able to grasp your toes which, not so long ago, seemed to be completely beyond reach.

After you have taken a short rest, sit up again in the same Head-to-Knee Pose to do the next exercise, which will eventually enable you to assume the Lotus Pose.

The Lotus Pose

As a preliminary exercise, place your left sole against the right thigh, then begin to make a bouncing up and down movement with your left knee as though it were made of rubber; the moment you push the knee down to the floor, up it bounces again. Do this bouncing in fast successive movements so that the leg resembles the wing of a flying bird. This will stretch and limber up the rigid ligaments and muscles and help you gradually to assume the Lotus Pose. First bounce the right knee, then reverse legs and bounce the left knee.

A variation on this bouncing is done as follows: Keep the right foot *on* the left thigh instead of placing it against the thigh, then start bouncing the right knee, as shown in the pic-

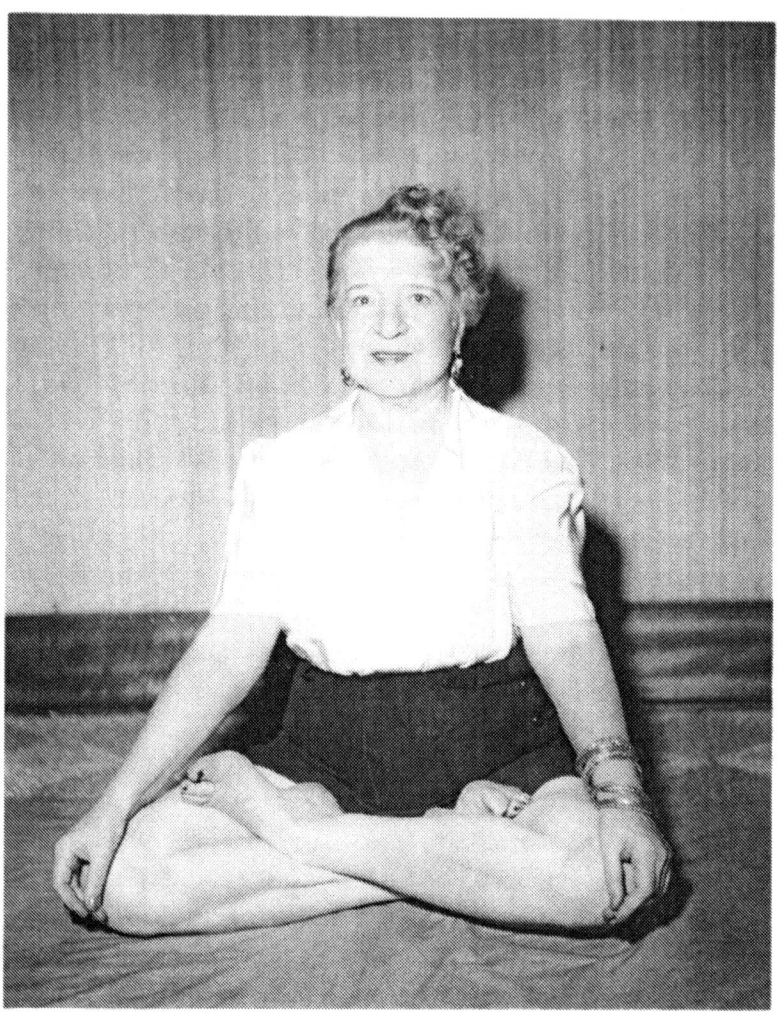

The Lotus Pose, or *Padmāsana*, demonstrated by the writer's mother, who is seventy-seven years old.

ture on page 25. If the bouncing knee easily touches the floor, then bend the left knee, take hold of the left foot with both hands, gently glide it *over* the crossed right leg and place it on

First Week

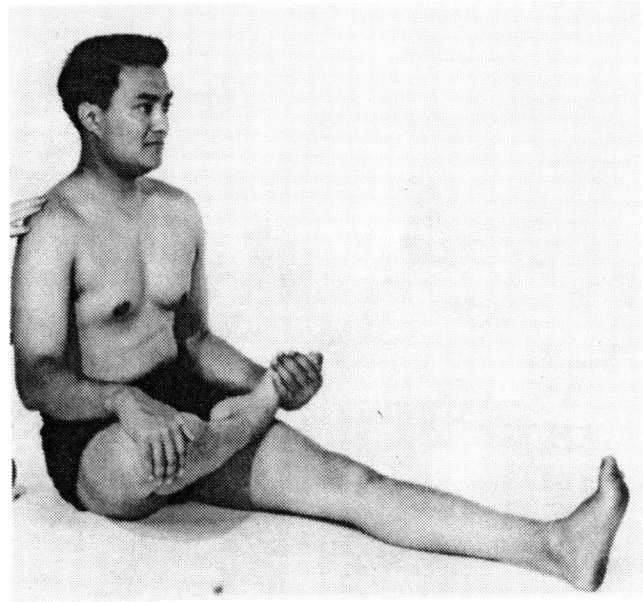

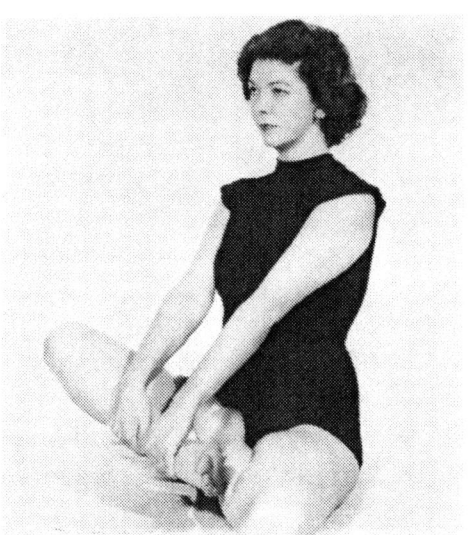

Practice for the Lotus Pose: (*a*) Place right foot on left thigh; start bouncing right knee until it touches the floor. (*b*) Next, bend left knee, grasp left foot with both hands and glide over right leg. (Photo by John Field)

Gloria Swanson relaxing in the Lotus Pose. (Photo by Miller)

the right thigh. Now both legs are symmetrically crossed and you are sitting in the Lotus Pose.

The hands should be kept on the knees with the palms open, and the thumb and second finger of each hand should touch, forming a letter O.

It often happens that new pupils, who had never suspected they could do it, are able to assume this posture during their first lesson. But mostly it takes time before people are able to master the Lotus Pose. So keep on practicing the knee bouncing daily until eventually your knee does hit the floor. This will be a sign that your legs are sufficiently limber for the Lotus Pose.

The Lotus Pose, or *Padmāsana*, is one of the basic Yoga postures. The others are the Headstand, the Shoulderstand, the Plough, the Cobra, the Twist and the Stretching Postures. There are also the Stomach Lift, *Yoga Mudra* and the Reverse Pose. The last two are not called Asanas, or postures, but *Mudras*, meaning gestures, while the Stomach Lift is called *Uddyiana Bandha—Bandha* meaning restraint or contraction.

For thousands of years the Padmāsana has been assumed in India not only by the rishis and yogis, but by ordinary people as well. Because of its calming effect upon the mind and the nerves, it has become a classical pose for concentration and meditation. Many Indians, especially in the South, also habitually sit in this pose when working, reading, writing or eating. It makes it easy to keep the spine erect, which as I have already said is a must. In the West, the Lotus Posture is often called the Buddha Pose, since most paintings and sculptures of the Enlightened One represent him seated in the Lotus Posture, with the hands on the knees or on the upturned heels.

In India one often sees people in deep meditation sitting motionless in this posture for hours. It has no special therapeutic value except to keep the joints in flexible condition and hold the spine erect, which is necessary for the breathing practices. It also helps develop a good posture.

The Cobra Pose

The posture you are about to do next is called Cobra, or *Bhujangāsana* in Sanskrit. It belongs to the basic group of Yoga postures. You will find it easy to assume, especially if your back is not too stiff and rigid. Even if your back is not limber you will be able to do the Cobra, though not perfectly at first.

TECHNIQUE: Lie down on the abdomen with your chin touching the ground; place both palms on the floor, or rather on the

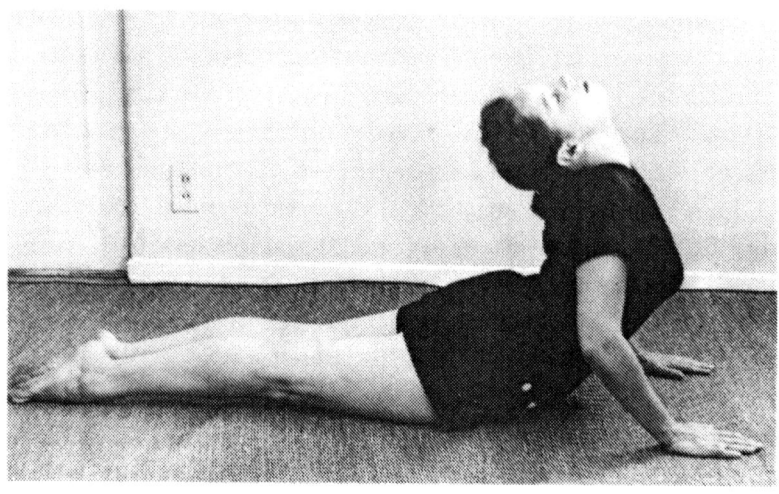

The Cobra Pose, or *Bhujangāsana,* stimulates the adrenal glands. Recommended for backache, gas pains, and ovarian and uterine disorders. (Photo by Jim Buhr)

exercise pad, at shoulder level. Keep your elbows high off the floor, legs straight, toes pointed, feet together.

Now while inhaling a deep breath, slowly raise the head, then the shoulders, chest and upper part of the body—the lower part of the abdomen should remain on the floor. Hold your breath and keep arching the spine until you feel strong pressure in the lower part of the back. *Do not straighten* the elbows; they must stay bent. Remain in this posture for a few seconds. Then begin to exhale, gradually lowering the body until the chin touches the floor again. Repeat once more and relax.

TIME: Keep the pose for two seconds, gradually increasing to ten seconds, and do it from two to seven times, adding one time every 14 days.

BENEFITS: The Cobra Posture affects the adrenal glands which are situated above each kidney, sending them a richer supply of blood. This posture is also beneficial for backache due to overwork or long hours of standing. It adjusts displace-

First Week

ments in the spinal column and tones the sympathetic nerves. It is an especially good exercise for women suffering from ovarian and uterine troubles. This posture is also practiced for development of body heat. People troubled by gas after meals will find the Cobra Posture to be very helpful.

CAUTION: When bending the body backwards, be sure not to make any violent jerks, as this may injure some rigid muscle. Come up slowly, gradually, like a rising cobra or a sphinx. After finishing the Cobra Posture it is good to rest in a knee-chest position, with the back rounded to relax it after the strain of holding this position.

Squatting Pose

Now get up to try the Squatting Pose, called *Utkāsana* in Sanskrit, which requires no particular skill or preparation. It is only when the knees have become too stiff that one will meet with difficulties while doing it.

In the Orient, especially in India, the common people often sit this way. You can see them squatting on sidewalks and beaches, in doorways and railway-stations. Once a rich Indian who owned a graphite factory decided, after visiting England, to provide his workers with stools to sit on. A few days later, the men came begging for the stools to be removed: they felt much more comfortable squatting.

TECHNIQUE: *First version:* Stand with your feet about a foot apart. Take a deep breath, while rising on tiptoe; then, while exhaling, start lowering your body, so that eventually you sit on your heels. Slowly rise again to standing position, keeping the back straight.

Second version: Proceed as above, but without raising your heels from the ground. Then sit in the Squatting Position with the buttocks almost touching the floor, the body slightly bent forward and the thighs pressing against the abdomen.

A *third version* is much more difficult, as you must squat

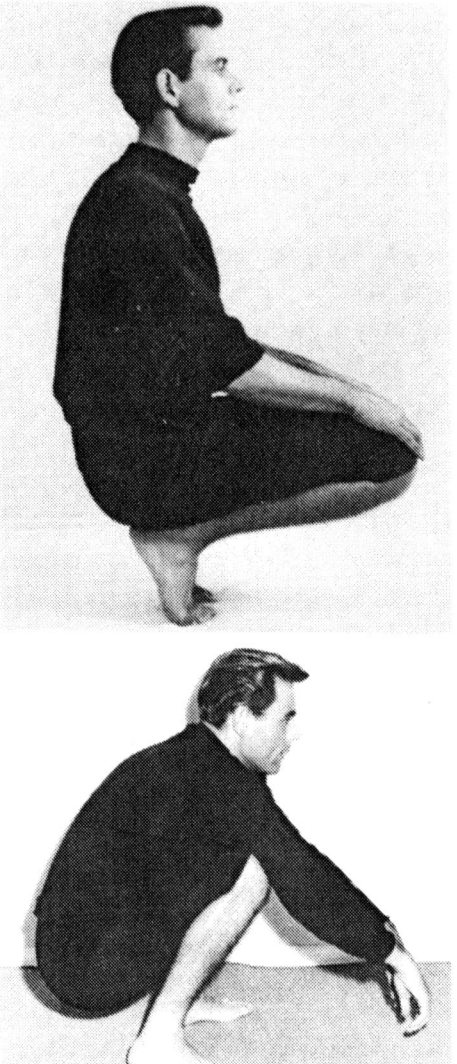

The Squatting Pose, or *Utkāsana*, limbers up stiff knees and helps improve elimination. (*a*) For first version, stand on tiptoe; lower the body until you sit on your knees with the back straight. (*b*) For second version, keep heels on the ground; balance by tilting body slightly forward, abdomen pressed against thighs. (Photos by Jim Buhr)

First Week

while keeping the feet close together, but *without* raising the heels off the ground.

Repeat any of the variations three or four times or do each one once. Then lie down to take a few deep breaths.

If your knees have lost their flexibility and you are unable to lower the body to the Squatting Position, start doing it by holding on to a door knob with both hands (open the door and grasp the knobs on both sides), or grasping the arms of a heavy chair or anything else that will hold your weight without toppling over, such as a piano, a bed, a sofa or a pillar. Gradually squat lower and lower down, making little swinging movements. In a few days you will be able to squat better.

This posture helps to limber up stiff and aching knees and to get relief from lumbago. It makes stair-climbing very easy and is a good exercise for skiers and mountaineers.

These, however, are not the main reasons for teaching you this exercise: one should learn to squat for better elimination. This position has been designed by nature itself as the correct posture for evacuation of waste matter, because of the spine being slightly bent forward and the thighs pressed against the abdomen. The use of high-seat toilets in the West is probably largely responsible for multiplying the number of sufferers from poor elimination and constipation. And these conditions in turn are directly or indirectly causing a host of other troubles and diseases.

There is but one disease, according to the world-famous surgeon, the late Sir W. A. Lane: insufficient drainage—inadequate elimination of poisonous waste material. Unless it is thrown off, poisonous waste remains in the system and begins slowly to undermine the health of our organism, finally destroying it.

A governess of my friend's children taught all of them to use the squatting position on the toilet seat, having observed that she herself never had any elimination problems in France where in their home they had a floor-level toilet without a seat.

They have floor-level toilets in India and Japan too, by the way, except in houses built for foreigners.

Not an aesthetic matter for discussion, it is nevertheless one of paramount importance for our well-being, and therefore should not be treated negligently or joked away.

The Squat is your last posture for today. You should not overtire yourself, especially since this is your first lesson.

BREATHING EXERCISES

You will now learn two breathing exercises. The first is very beneficial for people suffering from asthma. The second is especially good for those having sacroiliac troubles.

First Breathing Exercise

Lie down flat on your back and place your feet up on the wall as high as possible; stretch the arms out above your head keeping the elbows straight. Now do deep breathing while remaining in this position. Start with four deep breaths, then gradually increase the number. You may do this exercise even while lying in bed. Incidentally, people suffering from asthma will benefit greatly from this breathing exercise.

Second Breathing Exercise

Stand straight, feet together, hands at your sides, keeping the spine very erect. Cross the right foot over the left one, keeping toes on the floor, but the heel off, and the back part of the right knee on top of the left knee cap. Don't straighten the knees, and don't move the body to the left—it is important that it remain *with the spine centered.*

Now take a deep breath. While exhaling, bend forward until

First Week

fingertips touch the floor or come as near touching as you can manage. Return to standing position and take a deep breath.

Do this exercise three times, then reverse the legs and feet and repeat. When bending forward, be sure *not* to move the buttocks or shoulders. The bending should be done by the spine alone, starting from above the waistline.

If done correctly, this exercise removes the "morning" backache. People suffering from sacroiliac troubles should do this exercise twice a day to get relief.

RELAXATION

Your lesson for today is over and you will finish it with a period of complete rest and relaxation.

First, relax your hands by loosely shaking them a bit as if trying to shake water drops from your fingers. Do the same with your right foot, then with your left foot. Now stretch your hands above your head as if trying to reach for the sunrise on tiptoe and stretch as high as you can.

Next, let your body gradually become limp and heavy; pretend you are a drooping, long-stemmed water lily, and slowly sink to the floor. Lie down and close your eyes. This lifeless pose is called *Savāsana* in Sanskrit.

Now concentrate on the tips of your toes: relax them by withdrawing all activity from them. In the same way relax your feet, then the legs, the thighs, the trunk, the back. . . . Let the feeling of relaxation gradually overtake the whole body. Relax your shoulders, your arms, your fingertips. . . . Drop your chin and let the lower jaw sag to relax the muscles of the face. Now try to feel you are so heavy you are sinking *into* the floor, still fully relaxed and completely at your ease.

Lie like this, quietly, for a while. Then take a few deep breaths and try to visualize a cloud—a soft white cloud drifting in the sky. Hold this image for some time, then dismiss it.

Now imagine that *you* are this cloud. You feel so light . . . so relaxed . . . just floating in the sky . . . passing another cloud . . . gently gliding along . . . above a green valley . . . a field . . . a forest . . . above a small lake in which you see your reflection. . . . How pleasant to be so gently airy . . . so free and happy. . . . You are just a cloud in the vast blue sky. . . .

Next try to dismiss *all* thoughts from your mind and make it completely blank and thoughtless, as if you were sinking into oblivion, into nothingness . . . fully relaxed . . . peaceful and quiet. . . .

Stay like this as long as you wish. Then begin slowly, very slowly, to stretch your body. First stretch your arms above your head, yawning deeply. Stretch the hands . . . the fingers . . . the shoulders . . . the spine . . . the legs. . . . Roll over on your right side and arch your back. Roll to the left side, arching once more. Again lie flat on your back or abdomen. Then, after a while, still yawning and stretching, *slowly* sit up.

You may now get up and go about your business. But in our classes we always finish the lesson with a period of meditation in which everyone joins, including those who have taken up Yoga merely to get rid of some extra weight, of premature wrinkles, constipation, tension, insomnia, and similar complaints.

We simply sit down in the Lotus Pose, or else cross-legged, close the eyes and take a few deep breaths. Then we sit very still, trying to direct our thoughts to the Infinite Light which is God, Truth, Love, and is beyond form, beyond our understanding. We try to realize that It is everywhere, both outside us and within us; that we, as human beings, are the carriers of the Divine Light here on earth, that it dwells in our hearts, that our bodies are the Temple of the Living Spirit, and that we should let this Spirit shine through our eyes, speak through our words, be felt through our deeds.

Then we send a thought of peace and love to all those around

First Week

us, to our family, our friends, those whom we love, those whom we don't love, to all living beings on this earth and beyond. At the end we all say aloud:

> *From the unreal to the Real,*
> *From the darkness to Light,*
> *From death to Immortality*
> *OM*
> *Shanti, shanti, shanti.*

OM is the sacred sound of the Hindus, and *Shanti* means peace in Sanskrit.

You may also say any other prayer, or use your own wording—this is up to you. But I suggest that at least once a day you remind yourself that you are of divine origin and that you are on this earth to bring love, peace, and goodness to all living creatures.

GENERAL RULES AND SUGGESTIONS

Let us now recapitulate your first lesson item by item.

While still in bed you did the alternate stretching of the legs.

Then you learned how to do deep breathing.

Next you did the neck and the eye exercises.

Then came the Rocking exercise, the Raised-Legs Posture, the Head-to-Knee Posture, the preparatory exercise of knee bouncing for the Lotus Pose, the Cobra, the Squatting Posture, the two breathing exercises, and finally, relaxation.

If you have never done any exercises before, or have not been doing any for a long time, it is advisable the first day to start only with the breathing, the neck and eye exercises, one or two postures and relaxation. Then gradually, day by day, add the remaining postures, taking care not to overtire yourself.

Now let us go over the general rules and suggestions regarding your exercises and hygiene.

(1) Always do the exercises on an empty stomach; allow three to four hours after meals, one-and-a-half to two hours after breakfast or light refreshment. Never exercise when the bladder is full. Never eat immediately after the exercises, but wait for about half an hour before taking a meal. This is especially important if you have been doing strenuous exercises for an hour or so.

(2) Exercise in a well-ventilated room or in the open air.

(3) Do not exercise for more than fifteen to twenty minutes during the first few days.

(4) Rest frequently between exercises.

(5) Actual exercise time, after the first three weeks, should not exceed an hour.

(6) Don't wear tight clothes while doing the exercises.

(7) The Yoga postures are always accompanied by deep breathing, which is done with the mouth closed.

(8) After any long illness, resume the exercises slowly. For the first few days do only the breathing, relaxation, and neck and eye exercises.

(9) The same rule holds for women during the days of their monthly periods.

(10) One should refrain from doing the more strenuous exercises after the third month of pregnancy.

(11) Don't feel concerned if the exercises should produce a sense of fatigue during the first few days. This tired feeling will soon disappear. It is usually caused by over-toxicity. Merely take a rest without trying to fight off this fatigue.

(12) Take good care of your teeth. Rinse the mouth after every meal; cleanse your tongue as well.

(13) Internal cleanliness is *most* important for maintaining good health. Keep your body free of poisons by drinking plenty

First Week

of water between meals—but never ice water—and by taking an occasional enema, even if you are not constipated.

(14) In order to get rid of toxic waste matter, it is advisable to take an enema the morning (or the evening) before you begin this home course. One of the most effective cleansers for this purpose is a honey or a coffee enema.

Prepare the honey enema the following way: Dissolve three full tablespoons of honey in a quart of water at room temperature. Retain the enema for ten to fifteen minutes.

The coffee enema is made as follows: To a quart of boiling water, add three tablespoons of ground coffee. Do not use instant coffee. Boil for three minutes, then simmer another twelve minutes. Strain. Cool to room temperature. Take the enema and hold it for ten to fifteen minutes.

This may sound strange to you, but coffee when introduced through the colon does not react on the nervous system. Instead, it stimulates the solar plexus and liver secretions by affecting the adrenal glands and the gall bladder. It also activates the mucous membrane of the colon and thus helps to eliminate the accumulated toxins. A coffee enema would therefore also help to arrest the beginning of a cold or to stop a toxic headache. It is best *not* to take a coffee enema late in the evening, however, to avoid being kept awake at night.

(15) Do not sleep with a light in your room.

(16) Sleep in a well-ventilated room, with windows open, if possible.

(17) Do not sleep with green plants and flowers in your bedroom, for they give off carbon dioxide at night, whereas during the day they give off oxygen.

(18) Sleep with the feet to the South and head to the North, that is, parallel to, and not across the magnetic-force lines of the earth.

(19) For most people, the best sleep is before midnight, so don't keep late hours.

(20) Sleep with as little clothing as possible, or still better, in the nude.

(21) Do not sleep on a soft mattress and with high pillows, as this doesn't allow the spine to remain straight.

(22) It is always advisable to check your heart, lungs and blood pressure before starting on the Yoga postures.

At the end of our next lesson we shall have a lengthy discussion on the problems of diet. Meanwhile it would be best if you cut down on fried, fatty and heavy foods, on liquor and on cigarettes. This last is advisable even though the ill effects of smoking are greatly diminished by deep breathing.

DISCUSSION ON THE EFFECTS OF BREATHING

In our classes we often hold discussions at the end of the lesson, on various subjects directly or indirectly related to Yoga.

As you already know, Yoga is both a science and an art of living, and therefore touches innumerable facets of our daily life, from cleansing the skin to cleansing the mind, from a broken ligament to a broken heart, from overweight problems to marriage and even delinquency problems. There are actually very few matters on which Yoga has nothing to say. I propose that in this book, too, after each of our lessons we also discuss some of these subjects, for they might be of interest or help to you.

We shall begin with breathing—the essence not only of all the Yoga practices but of all life. Breathing is the most important of all our functions, for without breathing we could not stay alive longer than just a few minutes. Yet most of us do not know much about the effect breathing has on our body and mind; still less do we know about the role it plays in unfolding the spirit within us.

Our blood and entire organism is composed of millions and

First Week

millions of tiny cells, and it is through breathing that oxygen is carried to these cells by the blood stream.

We have only to remember that not a single tissue cell can be built without red blood, and in turn, not a single red blood cell can be built without oxygen, in order to have a clear understanding of the paramount part that breathing plays in sustaining life.

Try comparing a single cell with a toy balloon: Inflated with air, it is firm and "young," ready to fly up to the skies. But let our balloon develop a leak and it soon loses its tone, begins to shrivel, and finally wearily sinks to the ground.

The same is true of the behavior of each individual cell in our body. Unless provided with sufficient oxygen it becomes depleted, tired and lifeless. As a result the whole body begins to lose its youthfulness and vitality.

The life and functions of each cell are sustained by oxygen which dominates the activities of the entire body. Oxygen is a vital factor in the composition of minerals, the maintenance of normal electrical potentials, the breakdown and disposal of waste material.

We ourselves are rarely completely aware of all these complex processes going on in our body day and night, year in and year out. However, we do know that all of them would come to a standstill without oxygen. It is therefore our duty to assist the organism in this unending task, and we can do this by learning how to expand our breathing capacity.

Oxygen is also essential to the proper function of each of our internal organs, of which the most demanding is the brain. The brain requires three times the amount of oxygen used by all of the rest of the body.

There are over five million mentally-retarded children in the United States. According to the late Dr. Philip Rice, who dedicated his life to the rehabilitation of so-called problem children, many of these unfortunate youngsters are the victims of oxygen starvation of the brain and their condition could be greatly improved by putting them on a program of correct breathing exercises. He also feels that these same exercises would be of equal benefit in many cases of juvenile delinquency.

In his excellent book *Building for Mental and Physical Health*,[2] Dr. Philip Rice states that the I.Q. of a child can be increased by enlarging his intake of oxygen through correct deep breathing. However, he strongly condemns the wrong kind of "deep breathing" (in which the upper part of the chest is raised) labelling it a "thoroughly pernicious method." This, incidentally, is exactly the type of breathing usually taught in schools, gyms and health-clubs.

An inadequate supply of oxygen gradually impairs the function of the organs, speeds up the aging process and results in weakness and ill-health of body and mind. A deep breather need not worry—he can protect himself against all of these troubles. But civilized man is a shallow breather. He uses only one-third of his lung capacity, the other two-thirds being seldom, if ever, used.

How can man then expect to think, to create, to work and live in full measure, if he never uses more than one-third of his breathing capacity? He cannot expect to receive adequate nourishment for his cell functions, no matter how well and how much he eats, because the various processes of nutrition demand oxygen for the proper molecular exchange between the nutritive elements and the tissues. Then the electrical powers become fully released and are able to produce a greater amount of the enzymes that sustain our life.

Dr. Max Jacobson of New York, who was the first to isolate enzymes in their pure form, is of the opinion that for the maintenance of healthy cell-life, for cell renewal and survival,

---

[2] New York: Comet Press Books.

First Week

proper oxygen metabolism is imperative and indispensable.

Getting the most out of one's body by supplying it with oxygen is like getting a nut out of a shell with the help of a nutcracker. Therefore, if you want to have a good digestion, do not neglect the deep breathing that provides the organism with additional oxygen. The same advice holds for smokers. Talking to them about the possible dangers of excessive smoking is of no avail. They are probably more familiar than I am with all the literature linking cigarette consumption to cancer of the throat and lungs. Their raucous coughing alone should be a warning signal that something is wrong. But taking five or ten deep breaths after every cigarette would at least ventilate their otherwise permanently congested and clogged lungs.

The yogis, having recognized for several thousand years the tremendous power of breath, have successfully worked out an unsurpassed technique of utilizing this power for man's good. Deep breathing, as taught by them, can work wonders on tired, sick, and aging bodies and on restless, strained, and fearful minds.

Tension, sleeplessness, indigestion, constipation, nervous headaches, heart conditions, as well as mental abnormalities—including delinquency—are often the results of oxygen starvation. Unfortunately, the importance of deep breathing has not yet been fully recognized by most authorities, whether at home, in school, in hospitals, courts or prisons.

Even doctors seldom seem to realize how much of their patients' health and well-being depends upon their habits of breathing, although oxygen tanks are rushed to bedside in cases of emergency, when a person suffers a stroke or a heart attack.

Interesting observations on the results of oxygen starvation have been made by an Englishman, Frank Totney, who in his little book *Oxygen, Master of Cancer* voices the opinion that cancer is caused by oxygen deficiency in diseased cells that start rapidly multiplying in order to get sufficient oxygen. Whether he is right or not I am in no position to judge, but I do know that his ideas for cancer prevention very closely resemble the Yoga principles of breathing, diet, exercising and hygiene. Just like the yogis, he believes in the necessity of keeping the body internally clean by means of deep breathing, drinking more water (one glass for every 14 pounds of our body weight each day), eating plenty of fresh fruit, salads, and vegetables and purifying the colon by taking enemas about twice a month or so. In short, his idea is to rid the system of the accumulated poisons that are the direct cause of most of our ailments.

As man begins to advance in years, his life forces begin to slacken and he comes closer to the influence of the mineralizing earth forces. The cells of his body become less elastic, losing their ability to absorb oxygen the way they did before. Hence the body begins to shrivel, or else grows fatter and stiffer, and the organism is less capable of coping with all the work and the emergencies we expose it to.

A sufficient amount of oxygen is simply a *must* to prevent physical and mental deterioration and the kind of old age most people are afraid of—an old age that is reckoned not so much by the number of years one has lived as by deterioration of the functioning of the body's organism and of one's mental faculties. But so long as a human being does not know how to control his breath, he cannot ever expect to become master of his body or of his mind—he will always remain their slave. Even a common cold, for example, can turn an otherwise brave, fiery, cocky man into a pitiful creature like a chicken on a rainy day. We literally can, if we know how, breathe away most of the ills, tension, fatigue and other troubles we are heirs to, from a lack of self-confidence to a lack of confidence in God.

As we have already said, centuries ago the yogis worked out the most complete and elaborate science or art of breathing ever known to man. By using it, they have become capable of developing astounding, seemingly supernatural faculties and powers, over and above their ability to keep their bodies young, strong and free of disease.

But even an ordinary man, not only a yogi, can gain a certain amount of control over his body and his mind by means of deep rhythmic breathing.

Breathing, incidentally, is our only direct contact with the outer world, as everything else comes to us as impressions through the senses. Since breath is of cosmic nature we can, by using it consciously, establish a contact between Earth and Cosmos within our own body.

All this does not happen overnight, of course. Steady and diligent work is required in order to achieve such results. Most Yoga practices, especially the advanced ones, are based on the mastery of various breathing techniques. The majority of them, however, are ill suited to the Westerner and it is therefore best not to go into them in order to prevent possible dangers or even disaster.

A couple from Seattle recently came all the way to Los Angeles to see me because they had gotten into trouble by attempting *Pranayama*. Here is a direct quote from their letter, which tells its own story:

> We found a young Hindu, a University student, from whom we took five lessons. We were getting along splendidly until we started practicing Pranayama under his direction. Since then we have both felt miserable. In your book, *Forever Young, Forever Healthy,* you have rightly warned against practicing Pranayama.

This, I believe, should serve as an urgent warning to others.

To master the advanced stages of Yoga requires long years of special preparation and training under conditions difficult to approximate within the limitations of the present day American mode of life. Therefore, we should limit our attention to the practice of deep breathing, and especially rhythmic breathing, as this also increases the circulation and the flow of that mysterious life-energy which in Sanskrit is called *Prana,* meaning *Breath, Absolute Energy.* This subject, however, we shall not discuss until later, at the end of your fourth lesson.

Meanwhile, in the next lesson we shall deal with the values of nutrition, and give you an idea of how to ward off the aging of the body organism and preserve its youthfulness by learning to select the right kind of foods.

Lesson Two

SECOND WEEK

Physical control is merely a preparation for mental control; only when the mind calms down does the process of becoming one with the Reality begin.

A WEEK SHOULD NOW HAVE GONE BY SINCE YOU STARTED YOUR first Yoga exercises, and you may have already noticed their effect—provided, of course, that you have been doing them regularly. Let us check and see whether you can detect any results so far.

Are you sleeping better, or falling asleep more quickly? Has your elimination improved? Do you feel more relaxed, experience a sense of lightness? Are your personal problems a little less nagging than they used to be?

On the other hand, your habitual aches and pains may have increased, your limbs grown stiffer, your body more bloated. Perhaps you feel drowsy and sleepy all day long. If this happens to be the case, please do not get alarmed. In certain rather rare instances students of Yoga do experience discomfort in the beginning, and I always make it a point to warn my own pupils that a change for the worse may occur during the first few weeks of exercises. But this is nothing to worry about.

Some people go "down" before they can start going "up." Especially if the organism is in a very toxic state, the poisons which exercise stirs up make themselves felt. It is like shaking a glass of water with sand settled on the bottom—the water gets muddy before it can be strained and the sand eliminated.

So do not feel discouraged should this be happening to you, but give your system a chance to go through the cleansing process. You will feel like a new person afterwards. I remember one of my new students actually crying with pain in class while she was doing her exercises. She didn't give up, however, and as a result she is now free of arthritis, asthma, and sinus, all of which had been plaguing her. My own initial experience with Yoga was equally unpleasant. You may recollect that in the autobiographical notes in my previous book I mentioned how I swelled up instead of slimming down, until I could hardly get into my clothes, in spite of taking very little food. That, of course, was at a time I was not yet wearing saris exclusively, as I do now.

As suggested in the general rules in the first lesson, you should help the body to get through the cleansing process faster by drinking plenty of water and taking a daily enema for about a week.

Regarding the performance of the Asanas, I suggest again that you re-read all instructions carefully at this point and check whether you are doing the exercises properly or whether you have injected your own interpretations and are improvising without being aware of it.

Do not forget to do deep breathing with every posture and do not hurry any of the exercises—*do them SLOWLY!* Avoid being like the old lady I once knew who allotted herself fifteen minutes every morning for her exercises, rushed through them at whirling speed, immensely pleased to have accomplished so much in so short a time, and then complained of being out of

Second Week

breath. When corrected and slowed down she was amazed at feeling relaxed and revitalized afterwards.

Before we begin our second lesson, let us first go over your exercise schedule. You must have worked one out by now and decided which time of day is best suited for your Asanas—whether morning, midday, or evening. As a matter of fact, it is also permissible to work out a divided schedule—for example, to do one set of exercises in the morning and the rest at night. I do suggest, however, that once out of bed, you always begin your day with Rocking.

After the Rocking is done, go over the new postures given for the current week, and then continue with those exercises from the previous week which you personally need most. For instance, if you have sacroiliac trouble, don't fail to do the breathing exercise with the crossed-over foot. If constipated, practice the Head-to-Knee Posture or the Squatting Posture, and also Yoga Mudra, which you will learn today. If you are troubled by a sore throat or bad tonsils, do not omit the Lion Posture, which is given in Lesson Three. For the rest, you can either choose those exercises you like best or do a number of them alternately, depending on the amount of time you have at your disposal. But under no circumstances should you skip the basic Asanas.

Now let us begin the actual lesson. Remember, the new postures which you will learn in this lesson are meant to be practiced every day for a week before going on to Lesson Three. Remember also that *they are meant to be added to last week's basic postures, not substituted for them.*

Last week we started with the alternate stretching of the legs before getting out of bed. This you should continue to do mornings or evenings, or both. You may add to it the Toe-Twisting exercise, which helps correct falling arches and even in some cases flat feet.

This exercise is very simple: Stretch out the toes of the right foot and then, without moving the foot, bend them downward, the way you would if you tried to pick up something from the floor with your toes. Hold the toes in this position for a few seconds, then relax them. Repeat this several times. Now, instead of bending the toes downwards, pull them upwards. Keep them in this position for a few seconds, then relax. Repeat this several times. Then repeat both exercises with the toes of the left foot. Should you get a cramp while doing these or any other exercises, simply massage the affected place a bit. The cramp soon will disappear. Ultimately you will be free of cramping altogether.

Once you are out of bed and have done the Rocking, which you are probably enjoying by now for its bracing, invigorating effect, we will go on to the Half-Headstand. This is a simple pose which will help you later on to do the full Headstand without much difficulty.

The Half-Headstand

Even if you have no intention ever to stand on your head, try this safe and easy upside-down position, which even babies take delight in doing. Small children probably know instinctively what is good for them. It is good not only for them but also for you and me and anybody else who cares to try it.

We shall come to the benefits of the full Headstand in our next lesson. For the time being just try the following: Get down on your knees, clasp your hands together, interlocking the fingers, and place hands and forearms on the floor, taking care not to keep your elbows too far apart. Then place your head, about an inch above the forehead, *on the pad—not on the hands—*cupping the palms so that the thumbs hold the back of your head. Now, keeping your head on the floor, get up from the kneeling position, and stand on your toes. Then take a step or two forward, bringing your toes that much closer to

The Half-Headstand, good preparation for the full Headstand later on. (*a*) Preliminary pose: Be sure your fingers interlock and your elbows are not too far apart for comfort. (*b*) Second step: Place head on practice pad, *not* on the hands. Use thumbs to support the back of the head. (Photos by Jim Buhr)

your head. Hold this partly upside-down position for several seconds while doing deep breathing. Then relax and lie down. This is enough for your first attempt.

You have just completed the easy version of the Headstand. Did you enjoy it? It really was not too difficult—probably easier than you imagined. Often the mere thought of attempting the Headstand seems terrifying to beginners. "Me! Stand on my head! Never!", I have heard repeated again and again over the years and in all the places where I have taught. Yet often there was a gap of only a few minutes between this "Never!" and the full Headstand actually being done. Here I must repeat, however, that you should *not* try this exercise more than *once* in a single lesson. You have a whole week's time to practice it before we try the next movement.

CAUTION: Never do the Half-Headstand if your blood pressure is too high (above 150) or too low (below 100); if you get palpitations when you attempt it; if you are troubled by constipation and are passing an excessively dry stool; if you suffer from pus in your ears or from chronic nasal catarrh; or have very weak eye capillaries. The Half-Headstand should also be avoided if you have organically defective pituitary, pineal or thyroid glands.

Yoga Mudra (Symbol of Yoga)

Having taken a rest after the Half-Headstand, sit up in order to do the exercise called *Yoga Mudra,* or Symbol of Yoga. In some English books it is also referred to as The Stoop.

The practice of this posture is considered very important for its spiritual value in the higher stages of Yoga training when the pose is maintained for as long as one hour or more. The physical effect of the Yoga Mudra is mainly internal purification, as it helps keep our system clean by promoting a good elimination. To do the Yoga Mudra you must first sit down in the Lotus Posture. If you are lucky enough to be able to assume

Second Week

this without practice so much the better, but for most Occidentals this posture presents quite a problem in the beginning. Don't let this worry you, however, as I shall give you an easy variation of this Mudra which you can practice until the time when you are able to do the Lotus Posture.

TECHNIQUE: Sit up straight, keeping both legs crossed tailor-fashion. Clench your fists and place them on both sides of the abdomen, a little below the navel. Now take a deep breath, and while exhaling bend forward as low as you can, firmly pressing the fists against the abdomen.

TIME: Stay in this position from five to ten seconds, holding your breath, then slowly straighten the back, returning to the original posture. Eventually you should increase the time to three minutes, adding one second per week.

In order to do the Yoga Mudra in the classical manner you should first assume the Lotus Posture. Keeping both hands behind the back, clasp the left wrist with the right hand, take a deep breath and *while* exhaling bend forward until your forehead touches the floor. Remain in this posture for a few seconds, holding the breath, then slowly return to the upright position. Take a short rest and repeat. As you keep advancing in your studies, you will find that you can hold the Yoga Mudra longer and longer. When you do, you no longer hold your breath, of course, but breathe deeply while maintaining this posture.

BENEFITS: The Yoga Mudra is an excellent exercise for people troubled by constipation, as it increases the peristaltic movements of the bowels. It also strengthens the abdominal muscles, tones up the nervous system and the colon, and massages the pelvic region. It helps men to overcome seminal weakness. In the higher stages of training it helps the awakening of the Kundalini, which is explained at the end of Lesson Four.

CAUTION: If you suffer from constipation, you should prac-

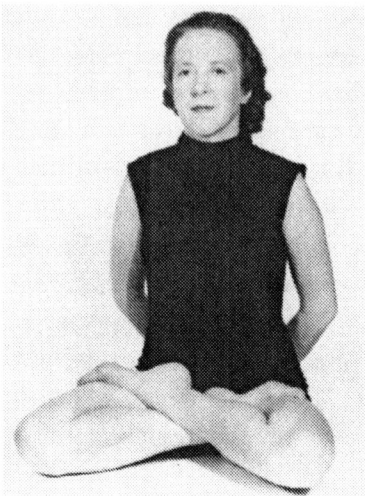
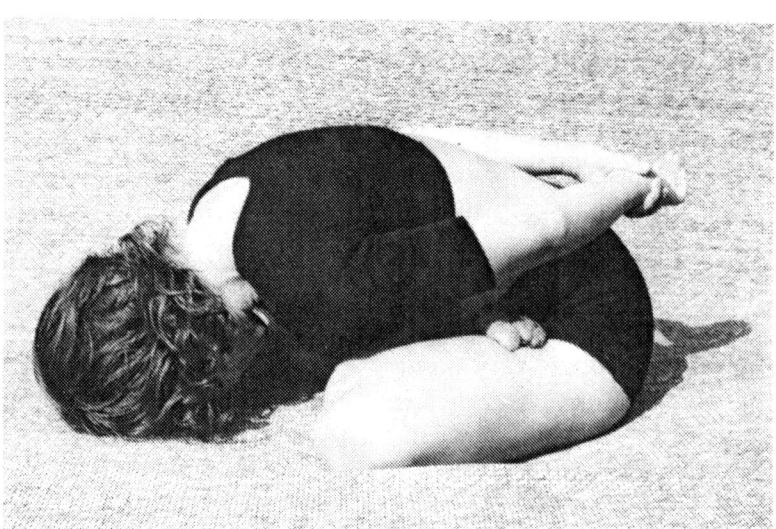

The Yoga Mudra, or Symbol of Yoga: (*Top Left*) Yoga Mudra may first be practiced tailor-fashion. (Photo by Jim Buhr) (*Top Right*) Traditionally, Yoga Mudra begins with the Lotus Pose. Posed by author. (*Bottom*) The Yoga Mudra strengthens the abdominal muscles, tones the nervous system, and awakens the Kundalini Power. (Photo by Jim Buhr)

Second Week

tice the Yoga Mudra very gently. Always release the posture slowly, without any jerking movement.

Lie down and rest before doing the next posture.

The Body-Raising Pose

We now go on to the Body-Raising Pose, or *Arohanāsana*.

TECHNIQUE: Start by lying flat on the floor. Interlock your fingers and place your hands behind your head, just above the neck. Take a deep breath, and simultaneously raise your head, shoulders and legs off the floor, keeping the knees straight. Maintain this posture for a few seconds while holding the breath, then exhale while slowly returning to the original position.

TIME: Repeat this posture once more. Increase the number of times, very gradually, from two to eight.

BENEFITS: This is an excellent exercise for strengthening the

The Body-Raising Pose, or *Arohanāsana*, excellent for reducing abdominal fat and relieving constipation. (Photo by Jim Buhr)

abdominal muscles, the pelvic region, the back and the shoulders. It helps reduce abdominal fat and relieves constipation.

CAUTION: This posture is rather strenuous and should not be done by women suffering from serious female disorders.

Bending-Forward Posture

After finishing the Body-Raising exercise, lie down and rest until your breathing returns to normal. Then take a few deep breaths before standing up for the next exercise, the Bending-Forward Posture, whose Sanskrit name is *Hastapadāsana* from *hasta*, which means hand, and *pada*, foot. You will notice its English name is not a literal translation.

TECHNIQUE: Stand straight, keeping the feet together and the arms hanging loosely along your sides. Inhale deeply and raise the arms above the head with elbows straight. Exhale while bending forward until you can grasp your toes with your hands. Get hold of the big toe by hooking it with the second and third fingers from inside and the thumb outside. If you cannot reach the toes, get hold of the ankles or calves. When exhalation is completed, press your head to your knees, keeping the knees straight. Hold this pose for a few seconds, then return to standing position and take a deep breath. Repeat this exercise twice.

Here is another version of the same posture. Place your hands on the floor, palms up, then step on your fingertips with your toes. Straighten, or try to straighten your knees, and press your head against them.

TIME: Hold this position for two to ten seconds. At first do it only twice but gradually increase up to five times.

BENEFITS: The Bending-Forward Posture is a very invigorating exercise. It gives lightness to the body, does away with sluggishness and with abdominal fat and relieves constipation and gas. It also gives a good pull to the sciatic nerves and hamstrings.

CAUTION: This posture should be done slowly, without any

Second Week

The Bending-Forward Posture, or *Hastapadāsana*, invigorates the entire body. (Photo by Jim Buhr)

jerkiness. After finishing it you can lie down for a moment, if you wish, or proceed with the next posture.

The Footlift Pose: First Movement

Next you will try the first version of the Footlift Pose. Its Sanskrit name is such a long one, *Ardha-baddha-pada-uttanāsana*, that we nicknamed it "The Stork."

TECHNIQUE: Stand up straight, then raise the left foot, bending the knees. Using both hands, place the left foot on the right thigh, as high as you can. Hold it with the right hand. Keep the knee down to the level of the right knee so that it does not stick out. Your spine should be erect. Stand steady on your right foot as long as possible and do deep breathing. Repeat the exercise with your right foot up on the left thigh.

To remain standing steady for as long as possible is easier said than done, of course. Usually during the first few days one does everything *but* stand still—hopping around on one leg and desperately trying to grasp for support. But it can be done.

The Footlift Pose, or *Ardha-baddha-pada-uttanāsana*, nicknamed "The Stork," is easier than it sounds or looks. (Photo by Mischa Pelz)

Second Week

Gloria Swanson, who, as you can see, posed for the illustration of the Footlift Pose, didn't have any difficulty in keeping still after only a few days of practice.

This, as I have said, is the first version of the Footlift Pose. At this stage it serves only to develop balance. In the next lesson you will learn the second movement of this posture. In the meantime, lie down and relax before going on to the next posture.

The Reverse Posture

Your next exercise is the Reverse Posture. In Sanskrit it is called *Viparītakarani Mudra* (pronounced Veepareetakārani Moodra). The Asanas, postures, are supposed to give strength, while the Mudras, gestures, are supposed to give balance and steadiness.

According to the yogis, within the human body, "The sun dwells at the root of the navel (the solar plexus) and the moon at the root of the palate." In the Reverse Posture the position is reversed and the sun raised above the moon.

TECHNIQUE: To assume the Reverse Posture presents little difficulty for most people. Simply lie down on your back, take a deep breath and raise both legs and the buttocks off the floor. While doing this, quickly put your hands on your hips to support the back. Keep your thumbs just under the hip bone and place your elbows on the floor about a foot apart. If the elbows are too wide apart they will not give adequate support to the body, which should be resting on them. Do not bend the knees. Keep the legs straight up and toes pointed, but without straining. Close your eyes and remain in this position while doing deep breathing, even if you feel a bit uncomfortable in the beginning.

TIME: At first, keep this posture for a few seconds at a time, gradually increasing its duration to about ten minutes.

BENEFITS: The Reverse Posture is known as a restorer of

The Reverse Posture, or *Viparitakarani Mudra*, known as the restorer of youth and vitality. (Photo by Jim Buhr)

youth and vitality. It is supposed to keep the glands, organs, and skin in a youthful condition, to banish premature wrinkles and prevent untimely aging. This posture is especially recommended for women who suffer from female disorders, irregular or painful periods and physical or mental discomforts during menopause. Manly vigor is also said to be preserved or restored

Second Week

First, sit on the floor with legs under a table.

Next, lie down flat, pressing the middle of the soles against the edge.

Using the feet for leverage, raise buttocks and back, keeping the elbows flat.

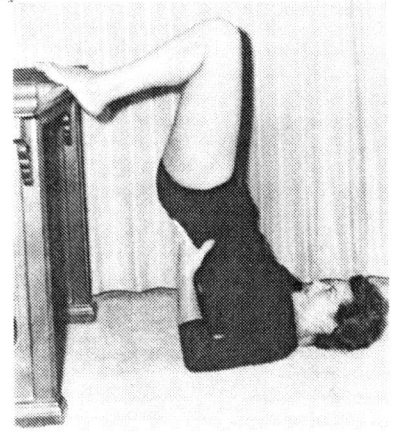

Practice Steps for Reverse Posture (Photos by Jim Buhr)

by the practice of this Mudra. It affects partly the thyroid gland, but mainly the gonads, or sex glands, which control the aging processes in our bodies.

The Reverse Posture is very popular in various beauty culture establishments and gyms, but there it is seldom, if ever, accompanied by deep breathing.

If you happen to be either afraid of doing the Reverse Posture, or are convinced that it is far beyond your capacity, try it first with the aid of a table, and you will be surprised to find that you can do it within a few minutes. Do it as follows:

Sit down on the floor with legs extended *under* a table and the forehead touching the edge of the table; now lie down on your back, raise both legs to the height of the table and press the middle of your soles against the table's edge, so that your heels are below the edge and the toes above it. Now raise your buttocks and back off the floor and support your body with both hands under the back, keeping the elbows on the floor. Stay in this position for a while and breathe deeply. Next try slowly to straighten first one leg, then the other. It will be easier if, until such time as you are able to keep them erect, you first sway your legs a little over toward your head rather than keep them straight up.

After finishing this posture lie down and take a brief rest. Then get up for the breathing exercises.

BREATHING EXERCISES

A Breathing Exercise for Good Posture

Stand straight with feet together. Put your hands behind your back and interlock the fingers, palms upward. Now turn the palms down. This will automatically give a twisting movement to your elbows.

Inhale deeply, then bend forward, while exhaling, at the same time raising the arms until they are stretched out. Do not

Second Week

bend the elbows, which should remain straight throughout. Keep your head down, trying all the while to swing your arms a bit higher and higher.

Remain a moment in this position, holding your breath; then exhale and return to the standing position without unlocking your fingers. Repeat the whole exercise two or three times.

Another version is done in a kneeling position, as shown in the illustration. The procedure is the same, except that here you bend over until your forehead touches the floor.

This is an excellent exercise for the waistline or a weak back, but even more for stooped shoulders. It should be taught to all children at home and at school to counteract their tendency to slouch, for slouching, in addition to being ugly, develops a bad and unhealthy posture as it prevents the lungs from expanding as they should.

If people could only see for themselves how ugly bad posture makes them look, they would quickly get to work to remedy it. This is especially true of women who wear swim suits and bareback dresses. I am reminded of an incident on the street in Honolulu, when I saw a lovely young woman in front of me take off her stole, suddenly baring a shockingly unattractive back with bones protruding like wings. A little later, at the beach, I received a second shock. The friends I was with prepared to go into the water, and I discovered that they too all had such "wings." Looking around, conscious now of the problem as a whole, I could see very few women or even young girls with really straight spines and a beautiful, dignified carriage. Later, up in my room, I promptly reached for a hand mirror to inspect my own back. It passed muster. Yet I am sure that years ago, before I had started on Yoga exercises, I would have been distressed by the results of this self-examination, since I too used to have the awful habit of slouching, much to the

The Breathing Exercise, done in kneeling posture: (*a*) Begin with the hands clasped behind the back. (*b*) This motion of body and arms is excellent for a sagging waistline, weak back, and especially for stooped shoulders. (Photos by Jim Buhr)

Second Week

chagrin of my mother who was always keeping after me to stand up straight.

Rhythmic Breathing

And now, before we finish our lesson with some relaxation, you will learn rhythmic breathing.

In India they say that by practicing rhythmic breathing you become attuned to the rhythm of the Universe; that by establishing a direct contact with the whole world you come to experience a sense of oneness with it. Then the feeling of separateness disappears and with it fear, loneliness, frustration, doubt, despair and other miseries.

Rhythmic breathing, as well as correct concentration and meditation which we shall discuss in our last lesson, can bring about a great change in both your physical and mental state and serve as a step toward spiritual unfolding. Through rhythmic breathing one also becomes aware of one's own rhythm. Each person functions according to his individual rhythm and when thrown off, whether by shock, a nerve-taxing job, strained family or business relations or any alien tempo, he loses his inner equilibrium. If the situation is allowed to continue, and a person does not regain his inner balance, he either becomes a nervous wreck or ends up in a state of collapse. The practice of rhythmic breathing could doubtless avert or remedy many such unhappy occurrences.

Rhythmic breathing can help you to acquire self-confidence, optimism, a calm mind or any other desired quality. The power one begins to develop with it is neither positive nor negative—it simply "is." It is up to us to use it for good or evil, and one must be very careful never to misuse it.

TECHNIQUE: Rhythmic breathing is done in the same way as deep breathing, but it is timed to the rhythm of your heartbeat. Inhalation and exhalation should be done to the same number of beats, as this establishes an even rhythm.

First assume the correct posture. If you cannot comfortably remain in the Lotus Pose, get into an easy cross-legged position or even sit on a chair. Remember to open your belt, unhook your bra, loosen your girdle or tie if you happen to be wearing any of these items. Keep the spine straight, with hands on knees, and start by taking a few deep breaths as you did before, and then stop.

Now put the second, third and fourth fingers of your right hand on the left wrist to find the pulse. Carefully listen to the pulse beat, and after a short while start counting 1-2-3-4 several times, to the rhythm of the beats.

Continue mentally counting 1-2-3-4, 1-2-3-4 until you fall into this rhythm and can follow it without holding your pulse. Then put your hands on your knees and take a deep breath while counting 1-2-3-4; hold the breath while counting 1-2; exhale while again counting 1-2-3-4.

Repeat this two or three times, no more. This is rhythmic breathing.

Should four beats prove to be too much for you, count three. Should it be too little, count five or six for breathing in, and the same for breathing out. When you inhale, do not merely stop at the end of the count before you have actually finished the inhalation: adjust the breathing so that both inhalation and exhalation become rhythmic. Always take an equal time for breathing in and breathing out.

TIME: You may repeat this exercise again in the evening, but do not overdo it in the beginning. Start with three or four rounds, adding one round per week until you finally reach the desired number, perhaps sixty or more.

Meditative Poses

You may also assume any one of the other meditative poses for your rhythmic breathing if the Lotus Pose is still too difficult for you. For instance, try the Accomplished Pose, called

Second Week

The *Siddhāsana*, or Accomplished Pose (*Top*) is often used by Yogis for meditation. The *Swastikāsana* (*Bottom*) is only slightly different. Both are recommended for persons who find the Lotus Pose too difficult. Posed by Bala Krishna. (Photos by Jim Buhr)

Siddhāsana from the Sanskrit word *siddha,* which means adept and accomplished yogi. It is done as follows:

Sit down with both legs outstretched. Bend the left knee and place the sole of the left foot against the right thigh so that the heel touches the perineum. Then bend the right knee and put the right heel against the pubic bone. Keep hands on knees with palms open if you do this between sunset and sunrise; after sunset reverse palms. The spine should always be held erect.

Here is another classic pose for meditation, called *Swastikāsana* in Sanskrit. Sit on the exercise mat, bend the right knee and place the sole of the right foot against the left thigh, the heel against the groin. Now bend the left knee and push the toes of the left foot between the right thigh and calf. Hold the spine straight. Hold your hands as you did in the Accomplished Pose.

Still another is the Symmetrical Pose, *Samāsana* in Sanskrit. The only difference between this and the previous pose is in the position of the heels: in Swastikāsana both heels press against the opposite groins, whereas here both heels should be set against the pubic bone—first the right, then the left. The toes of the right foot are pushed under the left thigh and the toes of the left foot are placed on the right calf, with the sole upturned. The spine and hands are kept in the same position as in the previous postures. If you cannot assume any of these postures, choose any comfortable position in which your head and spine will remain straight.

DIET

It is from the mastery based on the liberty to choose between the satisfaction of the appetites and the flight toward Spirituality that human dignity is born.

—LECOMTE DU NOÜY, *Human Destiny* [1]

The colon is the mirror of mind—when the mind gets right, the colon gets right.

—SWAMI PARAMANANDA, *Concentration and Meditation* [2]

No course in Yoga can be regarded as complete without the mention of diet, so let us here start our discussion of some of its most essential aspects.

We all know that next to air and water, food is most essential for keeping our bodies healthy, young and strong. Doesn't it then seem like a paradox to learn that America, the richest country in the world, is suffering from malnutrition, starving in the midst of plenty?

According to our leading scientists and nutritionists, one of the main causes for this is over-eating; the other is eating the wrong kinds of food. Our organism is nourished only by the food which it can break down and assimilate. Food which is not properly broken down turns into poison in the body. Far too much devitalized, unnatural, unwholesome food is being consumed by our population. The result is that our health picture looks sadder and sadder all the time. Diseases, especially degenerative diseases, are reaching such proportions that even people who are apparently healthy, or believed to be so, are found upon examination to be carrying one or another kind

---

[1] New York: Longmans, Green & Co., Inc., 1947.
[2] Cohasset, Mass.: The Vedanta Centre.

of illness which one day unexpectedly sends them into a hospital bed, onto an operating table, or into a grave.

We often hear that one or another of our friends has suddenly developed diabetes, asthma, coronary thrombosis; has been stricken with cancer, polio, arthritis or some other degenerative disease. We also frequently read in the papers about someone who has been taken to a mental hospital or dropped dead of a sudden heart attack in the prime of life—usually between the ages of forty-five and fifty-five—although apparently there had been nothing wrong previously. It seldom occurs to us that whatever happened was not really sudden, but in all probability the inevitable result of poisons accumulating over years of wrong eating and living habits. Reading such news may frighten us—yet what do we do about it? At best, we decide upon a physical checkup, but seldom, if ever, do we resolve actually to change our living and eating habits. In spite of the many warnings constantly appearing in various newspapers, books and magazines, not to mention health publications, we simply go along as we did before.

Let me here give just a few pertinent quotations along with my own and other people's comments:

Poor Diet Linked to Mental Illness
Improper Food Cause of Many Diseases, Nutrition Group Told.

Adequate diet is not only an effective remedy for any stress ailment but for much mental illness as well. . . .

The slowing down of the metabolic process (changing food into energy, tissue and body secretion) is caused by poor diet—too much white sugar and flour and not enough fruits, vegetables, meat and milk.[3]

Eating Linked to Gallstones

There's better than one chance in three that modern care

---

[3] The Los Angeles *Times*, May 20, 1956.

Second Week 69

can cure gall bladder trouble without surgery, according to the Minnesota State Medical Association.

The association said that the quiet daily control of diet, habits and exercise can accomplish a great deal for the one adult in five who has gallstones.

Burning up fat—

The materials which go to produce most gallstones are made when the body burns fat. In turn, the way the body burns fat depends on the glands, and the amount of fat it has to burn depends on the diet. If anything is wrong with either, gallstones are likely to form.

To stay clear of gallstones, the association suggests that everyone drink eight or more glasses of water each day, eat plenty of lean meat and avoid ice-cold drinks. Also avoid too much fried food, salad dressing, butter, oil and cream. Fruit three times a day is recommended.[4]

DOCTOR SEES DIET—CANCER TIEUP

... Dr. E. Vincent Coudry of the City of Hope Medical Center said that by reducing the intake of calories the incidence of cancer is also reduced. During World War II in Germany and other occupied countries the reduction of cancer cases was very marked because people were on low-calorie diets.[5]

It is interesting to note that Dr. Max Gerson, in *The Cancer Therapy*,[6] also speaks of fifty cancer cases cured by a special saltless, protein-free, fresh-vegetable, fruit-and-juice diet. He emphasizes that juice must be freshly prepared and consumed immediately, that is, not later than ten or fifteen minutes after it has been pressed, as otherwise it loses its enzymes—those minute particles which are the carriers of life activity in the body. And by the way, the juice of vegetables and fruit grown in organically-treated soil is immeasurably richer in enzymes than that from produce raised in chemically-treated soil. I have

---

[4] UP, Minneapolis, July 14, 1955.
[5] Chris Clauson in The Los Angeles *Examiner*, November 29, 1955.
[6] New York: Whittier Books, Inc.

seen this fact conclusively demonstrated by means of the Nemeoscope, so far the only existing instrument that is able to project on a screen the resolution of the enzymes and show them in their uniform structure and in action.

"Our Starving Teenagers" is the title of a dramatic article in the *Reader's Digest* of December, 1955, which has subsequently been reprinted for distribution in separate leaflet form. This article deals with malnutrition among teen-agers, which has become nation-wide. They fill up on the useless calories of the so-called "jitterbug diet"—a hot dog, a bag of potato chips, a candy bar and a bottle of pop—and they leave no room for wholesome nutritious food. The result: the health of the boys is so poor that the majority of them do not pass their army physical examinations. The condition of the girls, the future mothers of the nation, is still worse.

Worst of all, most of the damage is permanent. It affects not only the offenders but also their future children: "What a woman eats during the period of pregnancy and nursing directly affects the intelligence of her child." [7]

Another recent news item reads as follows:

ANIMAL FAT DIET BLAMED FOR HEART ILLS INCREASE

A diet high in animal fats is the villain in the mounting rate of heart and blood vessel diseases," according to Dr. C. M. Wilhelmj of the Creighton School of Medicine. . . . "A normal diet of a well-to-do family today is from fifty to sixty-eight per cent fat. Our diets have been going higher in fat content the last ten to fifteen years, so has our rate of heart and blood vessel diseases. [8]

When one considers that the daily food intake of a normal healthy adult should contain only about twenty to thirty per cent fat, including fats derived from eggs, dairy products, nuts

---

[7] Columbia Teacher's Report, released in 1955.
[8] AP, Omaha, Nebraska, March 10, 1955.

Second Week

and baked goods, it is small wonder that doctors are worried about the nation's eating habits.

An important factor to consider is not only the quantity of fat but also its quality. *Unsaturated* fats, mostly derived from plants and oils, are regarded as essential because they are low in cholesterol. The best sources of these are: saf-flower oil, sunflower seed oil, soya bean oil, corn oil and sesame seed oil.

The *saturated* fats, mostly derived from animals, eggs and dairy products, are regarded as unessential as they are high in cholesterol. Highest in cholesterol is brain, egg yolk and liver; the lowest is milk, cottage cheese and fish. All fruits and most vegetables are low in cholesterol.

Unsaturated fatty acids move about swiftly in our organism, whereas the saturated settle and become deposits. Professor G. J. Schoepfer, of the University of Minnesota Hospitals, Minneapolis, reports [9] that even *one* meal with too much saturated fat can cause a heart attack in a susceptible person. Also:

> At the 20th session of the American Academy of Nutrition Dr. Eugene H. Payne said that cooking fats like lard and butter which are popular in the United States, England, Sweden and Holland, cause in these countries more deaths from circulatory diseases than any other illness. "Excess fat leads to premature degeneration of the liver, heart, kidneys and blood vessels. . . . Putting on fat we must consider a serious metabolic disorder, no matter whether the individual still feels healthy or not. . . .
>
> "Fat is continuously in circulation; that is: some is put away in storage but, at the same time, storage fat is again put into circulation. Continuous turnover is a sign of health; with reduced turnover, metabolic disorder begins." [10]

I could go on and on like this, quoting report after report from newspapers, medical journals, magazines and books.

---

[9] *The New England Journal of Medicine,* December 26, 1957.
[10] The Los Angeles *Times,* May 21, 1956.

Their number is ever increasing. Yet in spite of these warnings most people still think that there is nothing wrong with their diet. "We always eat this way," they usually argue.

Probably because the damaging effects of an incorrect diet do not produce immediate ill results, we seldom blame our diet for our increasing ailments. How many otherwise well-informed persons would attribute a cold, fever, asthma, arthritis, polio, heart diseases and mental disorders to a toxic condition? Very few. Fewer still would stop overeating, or go on a cleansing diet or a fast, or practice deep breathing in order to get more oxygen when they need it to remain healthy.

For some curious reason, even constipation is rarely linked with faulty diet, although so many of our physical troubles originate in the stomach. Many of us might well join in a little prayer inscribed at the entrance to a 15th-Century cathedral in Chester, England, which reads, "O Lord, give me a good digestion, but also something to digest." But we in America should probably pray for fewer things to digest.

Dr. Ehrenfried E. Pfeiffer, Professor of Nutrition at Farleigh-Dickinson University, said in one of his lectures that to build and keep up good health, "one has to maintain a balanced diet which must be planned before the food enters the mouth." In other words you must first decide upon a menu, then stick to your decision.

It is not easy to suggest a diet that would suit everyone, since diet is a very individual matter. Much depends upon each person's physical condition, morphological [11] structure, weight, height, age, even one's occupation and mode of life. The food intake of a brain worker confined to his desk would, for instance, be inadequate for a physical laborer, while an expectant mother would hardly thrive on the menu of a dieting model. Moreover not only the amount but also the type of

---

[11] Morphology is the science of human structure and build.

food varies with the age of the individual. Both quantities and quality of food needed for a baby, a child, a teen ager, an adult, and an older person are completely different.

In Dr. Ehrenfried E. Pfeiffer's still-unpublished *Balanced Nutrition—Know What You Eat and Why*, we read that during the period of growth one needs more calories in one's diet, with a large amount of carbohydrates, which should be balanced. The adult between the ages of about twenty-five to forty-two needs a lower calorie diet, with fewer carbohydrates and more proteins, also well balanced. In the declining years one needs a diet low in calories and low in fat; good proteins should be prevalent.

But even within an age bracket there are fluctuations. There are people who are old at forty, others who just start living at this age. My own mother at seventy-seven looks and feels more like fifty-five. She does her daily Yoga exercises, including the Headstand, runs the household, dances at parties, and still has the clear, beautiful singing voice of a young woman.

In order to determine what to eat and what not to eat, you should study your own particular condition, then begin experimenting with various foods and combinations of foods to find out what suits you best. Remember, one man's food is another man's poison! Only, please don't turn into a food faddist who talks of nothing but his meals, his digestion, his elimination. And avoid the wrong kind of experimenting, like the man I once saw at a health lecture, who kept loudly agreeing with everything the nutritionist was saying while gorging on cheap candy bars. When, unable to suppress a smile, I suggested that he was doing the exact opposite of what the speaker was preaching, the man grinned sheepishly, showing a row of shockingly bad teeth, and said apologetically: "I am only experimenting!"

Health lecturers in this country have done much to make the public diet-conscious, but they are also responsible for creating considerable confusion with their contradictory theories. For instance, one of them will advocate drinking milk, while the next runs it down. One recommends raw foods; the next thunders against them. Still another is all for meat-eating while his colleague condemns it as ghoulish. And so it goes all along the line, until the poor listener is so mixed up he returns to his old—and generally bad—eating habits.

There are, however, a few "musts" on which almost everybody does agree. Personally, I learned them from my Yoga teacher in India. Here they are: Do not overeat; avoid dead foods; take plenty of fresh fruits, salads, and vegetables, or fruit and vegetables juices, provided you don't suffer from any ailment where raw food is prohibited; drink lots of fresh water during the day; finally, inhale a sufficient quantity of fresh air.

The best foods—those that are fresh, pure, clean and natural, such as vegetables, greens, fruits, whole grains, honey, oils, nuts, milk, eggs, fish and meat—contain all the necessary vitamins, minerals, amino acids and enzymes, the life-chemicals which control our metabolism. And metabolism, remember, is the rate of life.

The "dead" foods are those that have been robbed of their natural vitamins, minerals, amino acids and enzymes by processing of various kinds. They include everything canned, preserved, pickled, bottled, bleached, polished, refined and otherwise devitalized. White flour, white rice, and white sugar also belong in this category, since they have been bleached, polished and refined almost to nothing. They should be replaced in the diet by whole grain flour, brown rice and raw sugar—*not* white sugar mixed with molasses to color it, and then sold as "brown sugar."

Natural honey, obtainable from private bee-owners or from health-food stores is the best sweetener of all. The label will tell you whether it is unheated and unprocessed, "with nothing

Second Week

added and nothing taken away." Here is what German scientists have discovered about this kind of honey:

HONEY-EATING GETS SUPPORT

Bonn, April 7 (Reuters)—The West German Research Society has discovered that thousands of years ago Roman wrestlers were fed on large quantities of honey to increase their fighting power. Now they have heard that Russian athletes regularly eat honey for the same reason. As a result, the society is advocating the eating of more honey—only it emphasizes that it should be in its natural state, not honey which has been heated to make it keep longer.[12]

So much for honey. As for white sugar, the dental authority Dr. Melvin E. Page, in his book, *Body Chemistry in Health and Disease*,[13] describes for us how white sugar disturbs the sugar–calcium–phosphorus balance in the body. As a result it leads to dental decay. And while we are on the subject of tooth decay, let us mention that starches, too, help create favorable conditions for it by affecting the saliva in the mouth.

Another bad effect of white sugar is that it interferes with the maintenance of an even blood-sugar level and robs the system of Vitamin B. Long before the development of the Salk vaccine, in 1948, another medical authority, Dr. Benjamin F. Sandler, author of *Diet Prevents Polio*,[14] was able to check a polio epidemic threatening North Carolina by advising parents over the radio not to give children sweets in any form until after the danger was over. He had linked the consumption of soft drinks and sugar to polio.

White flour, which is concentrated carbohydrate, is converted into sugar in the liver. The bleaching and processing deprive it of its natural vitamins and minerals. Therefore all items made of this flour, such as bread, macaroni, noodles,

---

[12] The Los Angeles *Times*, April 8, 1956.
[13] St. Petersburg, Florida: The Page Foundation.
[14] The Foundation for Nutritional Research, 1951.

cake, biscuits, pies, soups, and gravies, have very little nutritive values and are mainly "empty calories."

In her book, *Feel Like a Million*,[15] Catharyn Elwood tells of a group of school children who were preparing an exhibit of mice for a fair in Long Beach. Some of the mice were fed on puffed wheat and some on whole-grain wheat. A few days before the opening, the puffed-wheat-fed mice died, and the youngsters thereupon refused to eat puffed wheat at home. Here was an example of visual education of a kind the advertisers don't bargain for!

Let me also mention an experiment made in school with a human tooth: The tooth was dropped into a bottle containing one of the most popular soft drinks. Within three weeks it had completely dissolved. Only then did the youngsters fully realize why the school authorities had prohibited the sale of soft drinks on the grounds.

At least one government I know of, the German, has forbidden the bleaching of flour; I am also told that the governments of Japan and China are considering the prohibition of rice-polishing. According to a sportsman from Finland, Russian Olympic team members owed their physical fitness to their wholesome food and special breathing exercises. In an interview given to the Swiss magazine *Volksgesundheit* in May 1954, this same Finn said that while he was trying to find out the real reason for the phenomenal success of the Russians in the Olympics, he began observing them closely during the games in Helsinki and Falun. A perfect knowledge of their language permitted him to engage in friendly conversation with his Russian colleagues and to spend a great deal of time with them. In his opinion, they had two great advantages over the other participants in the sports. First, they used a special breathing technique that enabled them to feel at ease

---

[15] New York: The Devin-Adair Co.

Second Week

while others were puffing and panting. The second was their healthy mode of life and *natural diet* consisting mainly of fresh vegetables, greens, fruits, and milk products. All these were of a quality unfortunately unobtainable in the "civilized" countries of the West, for fruits and vegetables in Russia are still raised in healthy soil treated with natural fertilizers, not with chemicals. They are also free of poisonous sprays and gases. Consequently milk, too, comes from healthy cows whose grass and fodder are not grown with the help of chemicals.

Vegetables grown with chemicals, incidentally, are overrich in potassium and too poor in magnesium; this imbalance produces toxicity in the human body. But the craze for systematically poisoning foodstuffs is still unknown to the majority of Russians. The interviewer concluded that his findings should lead not only all sportsmen, but also all other people the world over to do some serious thinking on the subject.

Judging from the *Volksgesundheit* article, the diet of the Russian athletes is very similar to that recommended by Indian yogis. Both give ample proof of the truly astonishing results of natural diet combined with special breathing techniques and a healthy mode of life and exercises. A shining example of this is the Hunzas [16] of India. These people have recently caught the attention of the world because of their exceptional good health and longevity. Men over a hundred years old are still strong enough to do heavy work and till the soil, and their teeth show no signs of decay. I myself have seen almost miraculous transformations and recoveries in people who have taken up the practice of Yoga postures and changed their food habits. This includes my own case.

On our pantry shelves at home you will never find anything canned, preserved, bottled, bleached, refined or processed.

---

[16] An interesting book, *The Hunza-Land*, has recently been written by Dr. Allen E. Banik, who has made a study of these people, their mode of life and eating habits. Whitehorn Publishing Co., Long Beach, California.

Whole grain flour is substituted for white flour; brown rice for white rice; honey for white sugar, for table and kitchen use, as even raw sugar is used sparingly. Cocoa and chocolate are also absent and carob powder substituted in desserts or beverages. Personally I do not care for desserts, and I generally drink coffee-substitutes made with raw goat's milk or soya bean milk, various herb teas, buttermilk, fresh vegetable and fruit juices, and plenty of fresh water with or without lemon. We also use lemons instead of vinegar. For seasoning we use all types of vegetable, mineral, and sea salts plus fresh and dry herbs, onion and garlic. Onions and garlic, by the way, were forbidden by my Yoga teacher for the duration of my training, just as were all other vegetables that do not ripen under the direct rays of the sun, such as beets, carrots, radishes and potatoes. For during the time of the discipleship a pupil must lead a sexless life and must therefore avoid all passion-exciting foods.

It goes without saying that as a Yoga disciple I was not to touch alcohol, cigarettes or meat, none of which made any difference to me, since I was already a teetotaler, a non-smoker, and a vegetarian. But I did enjoy coffee, which I also gave up, along with tea, chocolate and cocoa, because my teacher branded them as poisons.

Alcohol is avoided by the yogis because it lowers the vibrations of their astral body, whereas the purpose of Yoga is to heighten these vibrations. They do not smoke because it congests and poisons the lungs, and Yoga aims to cleanse the organs. Smoking is also supposed to coarsen and make breakable the astral web, which in a developed individual should be thin and strong enough to protect him from the lower influences. Meat is not eaten for several reasons. To begin with, the yogis don't believe in killing; moreover, the idea of eating a dead corpse is repulsive to them. The astral vibrations of the slaughtered animal have an effect on the astral body of the person eating the meat.

Second Week

One of our friends, a university professor from Europe, had to give up eating meat because he began to see the astral bodies of the killed animals he was about to eat. He told me, for instance, that oysters, scallops, and crabs, so rich in protein, were the worst for our own astral bodies and fish the least harmful.

You, however, need not exclude all these from your diet, since you are not subject to the strict disciplines of a Yoga aspirant, and can make your own decisions. If you are a smoker, however, at least do deep breathing exercises often to keep your lungs cleaner.

But in order to obtain better general results from following these teachings you should, for your own benefit, revise your eating habits. Every American would benefit by a more sensible and more balanced diet than his present one, for our eating habits are slowly but surely damaging the health of the entire nation. So if you are anxious to regain or retain your health don't neglect the following diet suggestions to which I personally adhere in my daily life.

(1) *Never drink iced water*, especially not with meals, as this interferes with the free flow of digestive juices and impairs digestion. The drinking of iced water is America's national sin against proper digestion.

(2) Drink a glass of fresh, pure water, at room temperature, the first thing in the morning and the last thing at night. It should be taken hot only when one is troubled by constipation. In that case a little lemon may be added. Hot water, or herb tea with lemon—and honey if you wish—taken on a hot summer day makes you feel cooler afterward.

(3) Drink five to eight glasses of water a day, or one glass for every fourteen pounds of your body weight. In those parts of the country where fluoride is added to the water, drink distilled water to be on the safe side. Even President Eisenhower is known, on occasion, to have carried his own drinking water.

Next to air, water is one of the bodily supplies most urgently demanded by nature. Eight-tenths of our physical body consists of water and we eliminate about two quarts of it a day. An insufficient intake of water is often responsible for constipation and a congested colon, for malfunction of the liver and kidneys, and for clogged bowels.

(4) Don't drink water *with* your meals, but take it a half hour before or two to three hours after meals, so as not to disturb the processes of digestion by diluting the digestive juices.

(5) Sip the water slowly, never gulp it down all at once.

(6) In order to restore to water the life-elements lost in boiling or processing, pass it through the air, pouring it from one glass into another several times. You will soon notice that this gives a slightly invigorating and stimulating effect, which is absent in lifeless and devitalized water.

(7) It is better to *eat* fruit than to drink fruit juices.

(8) When making fresh vegetable juices from carrots, radishes, beets, etc., add some of the green tops.

(9) Don't keep juices standing, as they will lose their precious enzymes. Orange juice, for instance, loses one third of them after a half hour, and all of them after two hours.

(10) Alcohol, tea, coffee, cocoa and chocolate are not recommended, because tannic acid, theine, caffeine and theobromine are stimulants.

(11) Milk is a food, not a drink. It should be taken in small sips, otherwise it is likely to produce indigestion.

(12) It is not the amount of food you eat that nourishes your body, but only the amount the body itself can assimilate.

(13) Choose carefully the foods that suit your system; choose them just as carefully as you choose a dress, a hat or a tie. At first you will have to experiment, trying various foods and various combinations, until you find out which suit you best.

(14) Avoid all devitalized foods such as canned goods, pol-

Second Week

ished rice, white flour and refined sugar; use unpolished rice, whole-wheat flour and brown sugar or honey instead. Try to cut down on candy, pastries and vinegar, cider vinegar excepted.

(15) Chew your food carefully, especially if it is the starchy kind, so that it may be properly mixed with saliva; unless converted into glucose by the saliva in the mouth, starch will lie putrefying in the stomach for several hours.

(16) Toasted or dry bread is better than fresh, *but do not eat bread together with any liquid*—let the teeth work on it properly. Better have whatever you want to drink *before* eating the bread, as starch should be converted into glucose by the saliva.

(17) Eat only one starch to a meal. For instance, if you take rice omit bread, potatoes, macaroni, starchy pudding, thickened gravy and so on.

(18) If you suffer from gas, it is advisable to plan your meals so that you do not eat starch and protein together, and especially not with cooked sulphur foods like peas, cabbage, cauliflower, eggs, turnips and so on, because gas is produced by sulphur working on the starch. (See the Hay Diet in Appendix I.)

(19) Don't throw away the water in which vegetables have been boiled, but use it for soup, gravies, or for drinking. Potato water is very good as it alkalizes the body. See recipe in Appendix I.

(20) Don't throw away the green tops of carrots, beets (beet tops should be first scalded with boiling water before being cooked), parsnips, radishes etc.; add them tied in a bundle to soup, then throw them away when the soup has cooked.

(21) Vegetables should be boiled in very little water over a slow fire, or better still without any water, in special vapor-sealing stainless steel utensils.

(22) Fried foods as well as rich dishes should be avoided

altogether, because these digest more slowly than fat itself. Fat is the last to leave the stomach, carbohydrates coming first and then the proteins.

(23) All saturated fats, like lard, margarine, eggs, butter and dairy products tend to increase the blood cholesterol level and can be classified as unessential fats.

(24) Highest in cholesterol are brains, egg yolk, and liver; the lowest are milk, cottage cheese, and fish. All fruit and most vegetables are also low in cholesterol.

(25) Any diet which is high in saturated fats is dangerous. So eat balanced meals: a high fat and low protein diet inhibits the function of enzymes.

(26) All unsaturated fats, such as oils, keep the blood cholesterol level low and can be classified as essential fats. The best sources are saf-flower oil, sunflower seed oil, soya bean oil, sesame seed oil, and cornflower oil. Cottonseed oil is not a good source.

(27) Remember it is not only the calories and the amount of fat that decides the issue of nutrition and health, but the *quality* of the fat. Bacon, for instance, has caloric fat value only. It contains nothing else, neither vitamins, nor minerals.

(28) The warming up of meals containing *any* kind of fat, oil included, renders them more and more indigestible with every reheating. Both deep frying and re-using fat left in the frying pan are not recommended either, for the same reason. Try to use only oils labeled "cold pressed," usually obtainable in health food stores.

(29) Any of the oils mentioned in paragraph 26 as well as old fashioned cod liver oil are very good lubricants for the system and a help to better elimination if taken at night; take one tablespoonful three or four hours after the last meal.

(30) Six glasses of fresh raw cabbage juice a day keep peptic ulcers away.

(31) One of the best strength restorers is the "Calcium Cock-

Second Week

tail." According to Professor Carl Albin, calcium, lemon, sulfur (egg yolk), honey and a little alcohol will restore the normal balance and activity of the gonads, or sex glands, within thirty to sixty days. It is prepared as follows: Put 8 raw eggs into a jar without breaking their shells. (The eggs should be fertile and must come from chickens that are allowed to run free. The commercially distributed eggs lack certain vitamins.) Cover with the juice of about 16 lemons, preferably grown organically without any poisonous spray on them, and keep in refrigerator for 4-6 days, until shells are dissolved by the lemon and reduced to powder. Take out the eggs, being careful not to break the thin membrane, separate the yolks from the whites which are not to be used, and put the yolks back into the bowl. Press its contents through a sieve or put into a liquefier, add raw honey to taste and pour in 2-3 ounces of brandy. Keep in refrigerator. Take a tablespoonful 3 times a day before meals, shaking well before using.

In spite of being a teetotaler, I must give this cocktail recipe in full—the brandy in it is supposed to extract the active ingredients. It also acts as a natural preservative.

(32) The richest source of protein is soya bean. Two pounds of soya bean flour contain as much protein as four pounds of cheese, or five pounds of boneless meat, or six dozen eggs, or fifteen quarts of milk. Soya bean is the only non-acid forming protein.

(33) The most essential rule about food, however, has nothing to do with its quantity, quality, or preparation, but with your mental attitude at the time you are eating it.

Aside from the fact that a meal should never be eaten hurriedly, it is most important that it be taken with enjoyment, in congenial company and with pleasant surroundings. Food eaten in a state of anger, aggravation or displeasure produces a toxic condition in the body. Therefore it is better to skip a meal when in a bad state and wait until one gets back to normal.

Try to make your mealtime harmonious by avoiding upsetting discussions. A nicely-set table also adds to the pleasure of eating. So does a smiling face, a cheerful word, a beautiful flower or a picture. Bless your food, and enjoy it.

Unpleasant news should never be broken at table or just before meals, as this upsets not only the digestion but the entire organism. You will know why even better when you come to the third lesson where we shall talk about "stress" and the "stressors."

Lesson Three

THIRD WEEK

Mind is the master of senses and breath is the master of mind. The mind cannot be restrained without restraining the breath—mental activity keeps pace with respiration.

The Headstand: First Stage

Now that you have been practicing the Half-Headstand for a whole week, you should be ready to try the full Headstand, or *Shirshāsana*. By far the simplest, safest approach for the beginner is to try the posture first in a corner, in order to have maximum support. When you attempt the Headstand this way, you need feel neither nervous nor insecure, for the walls afford protection on both sides and exclude the possibility of a fall.

However, you will need a helping hand to stand on your head the first time or two. You can safely ask almost anyone to help you, for no special skill is needed. One friend of mine, who lives alone and is the kind of person who hesitates on principle to trouble anyone, tells me she managed her very first headstand completely alone: she pushed an armchair to the wall close to the corner, then put her leg on the arm of the chair while practicing. This method sufficed until she ac-

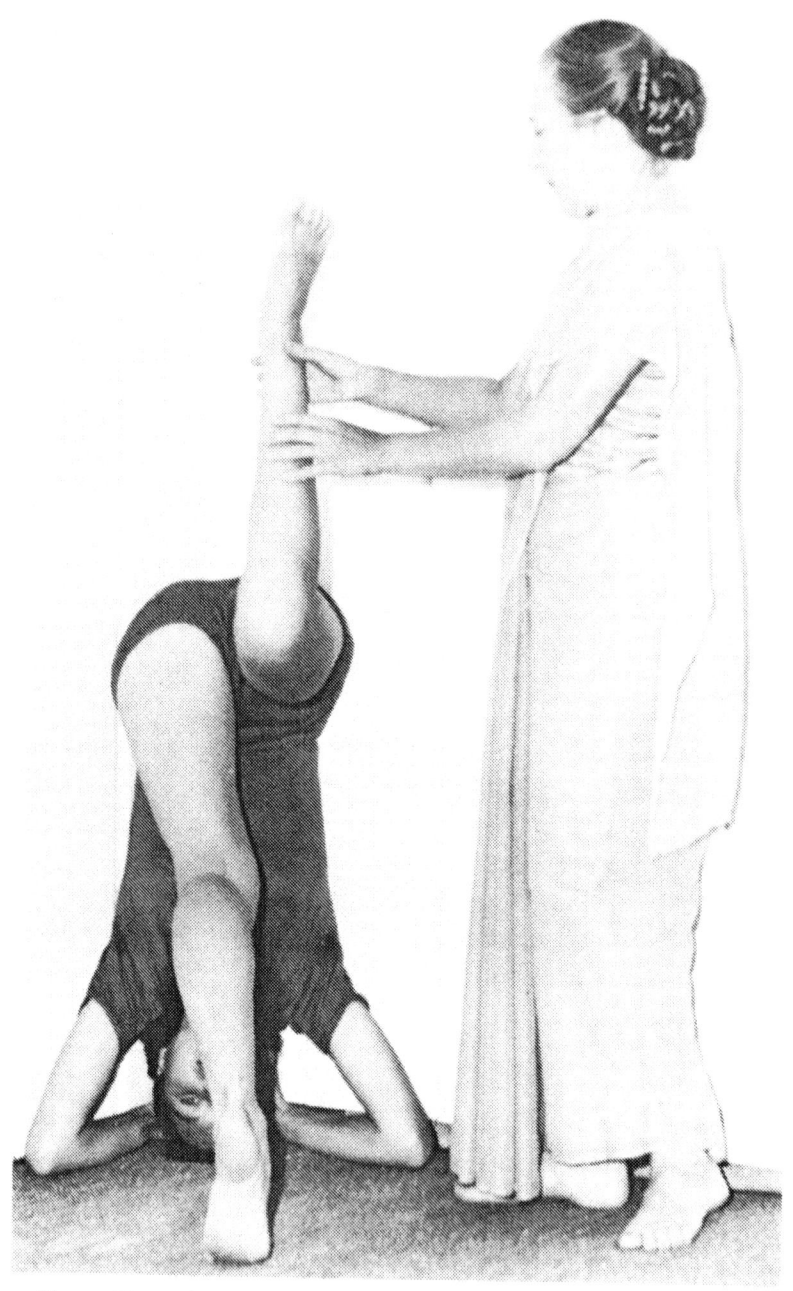

You will need a helping hand when you first try the Headstand. (Photo by Jim Buhr)

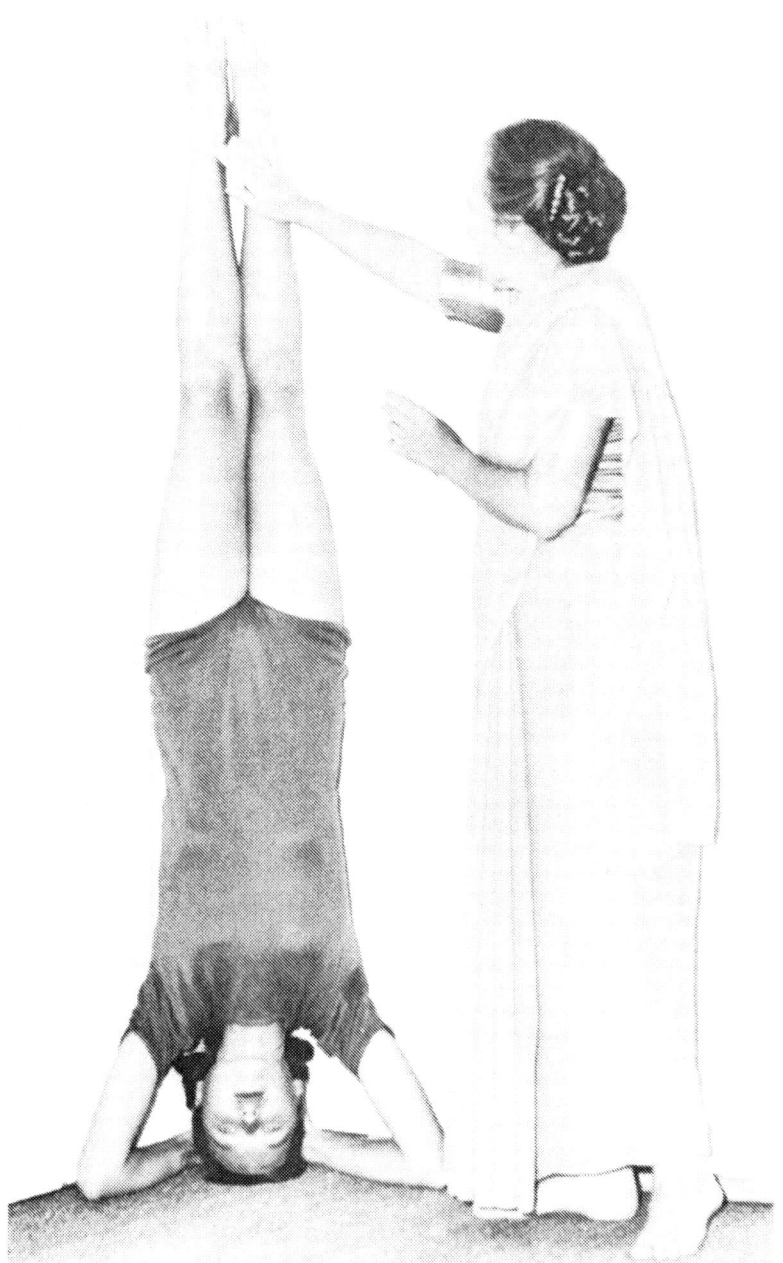

A corner is helpful until you have acquired a sense of balance.
(Photo by Jim Buhr)

quired a sense of balance and confidence. Here is the way to do the Headstand:

TECHNIQUE: Put a quilt or folded blanket in your corner, so that it fits flat: do not use pillows, as these are too soft. Now interlock your fingers, place them cupped on the blanket, and place your head in the hollow of your palms, "nesting" it there, about one inch above the hair line. Do *not* place the head *on* the fingers or palms: this is a mistake made by many people. Now get up off your knees and take a few steps toward your head, as in the Half-Headstand. Then raise either leg as high as possible and have whoever is helping you grasp it by the ankle. On the count of three, make a little jump, while he or she simultaneously places the raised leg in the corner against the wall. The other leg will follow of its own accord. Your assistant can gently place his hands against your legs to keep you from falling back. And that is all there is to it!

You are now standing on your head with both legs straight up, supported on either side by the wall. All you have to do is to relax: if you keep the legs stiff, the body tense, and the spine arched, you will feel so uncomfortable that it would be better to come down at once. Moreover, if you tense up your assistant will find it difficult to raise your leg up against the wall. Consequently, if you find that you are simply unable to relax, but remain stiff and tense, it is best to let a few days go by before attempting the Headstand again.

You should not hold the Headstand for more than fifteen seconds in the beginning; then come down slowly, first bending the knees, then lowering the feet all the way to the ground. Remember always to keep the toes inverted, otherwise you may injure them when you reach the floor. If you prefer to have help in coming down too—which is not a bad idea until you have mastered the technique—then bend only one leg while the person helping you grasps the other one by the ankle and holds it lightly, letting it follow the one you yourself are

Third Week

lowering. Make certain the manipulation is done gently, without any pulling, hurry, or interference with the natural tempo of your own movements. Your assistant, by the way, should be standing at your right if you start coming down with the left foot, on your left if you come down with the right one.

After you have come down, remain kneeling for a few seconds with your head on the floor; then stand up, raise your arms above your head, inhale deeply, and lie down to rest. After a while take a few more deep breaths.

The Headstand done this way represents no difficulties at all. A great many persons can do it at once, without practice. Just remember to keep the toes pointed, the body relaxed, the spine straight, the neck and shoulders free from tension, and the elbows not too wide apart; for the weight of the body must partly be carried by the forearms.

It is so easy, in fact, to stand on one's head in a corner that after a press conference I often have reporters and photographers successfully trying it right in my room. And once, after completing a television interview in Washington, D.C., I found myself giving a class in Yoga to a whole roomful of enthusiastic studio technicians who had been watching the program. Most of them were able to do the corner Headstand then and there, and did it with ease.

I must warn you, however, that using a corner to steady yourself has one disadvantage: you can grow so accustomed to this method that it may take you longer to start doing the Headstand without safeguards, in the middle of the room. As far as the benefits of the posture go, this does not really matter, of course. But the correct, classical posture should be done without any support.

TIME: Do the Headstand for fifteen seconds at first, adding fifteen more per week. The maximum time for it should not be more than twelve minutes, if it is done in conjunction with other exercises.

BENEFITS: The benefits of the Headstand are so numerous that it has been called the "King of Asanas. In the first place, it affects four of the most important endocrine glands—the pituitary, the pineal, the thyroid, and the parathyroids, glands that are responsible for our very existence, for they keep the body mechanism in good working order. As a consequence, the practice of the Headstand helps us to get relief from many of our troubles, physical as well as mental, or better still, to prevent them. Yoga recommends it highly for people suffering from nervousness, tension, fatigue, sleeplessness, dullness, fear, poor blood circulation, bad memory, asthma, headaches, constipation, congested throat, liver or spleen, for female disorders, the initial stages of eye and nose troubles and general lack of energy, vitality or self-confidence. But most important of all is the fact that it affects the pituitary, the master gland of the body.

In rare cases there are difficulties in the beginning. I once had a pupil, a prominent woman on a visit from New York to California, who was never able to do the Headstand because as soon as she tried it her nose would start bleeding. Some time later, when I saw her again in New York, we tried it again and this time she showed no ill-effects. She told me that in the interim she had been practicing other Yoga exercises; she had also been eating one or two slices of raw onion daily. Unable to decide what had been really responsible for her sudden success, we decided to split the credit. I don't suppose we shall ever arrive at an answer, and I give you the story without trying to draw too many inferences.

CAUTION: The Headstand should not be done by persons whose blood pressure is either very high—that is, above 150—or very low—below 100; by persons who get palpitations when they try it; or by those suffering from constipation, when the stool is excessively dry. It should also never be done by persons suffering from pus in the ears, from chronic nasal catarrh, or

Third Week 91

from very weak eye capillaries. Finally, it should be avoided by those with an organically defective pituitary, pineal or thyroid gland.

The Stretching Posture

Next you will do the Stretching Posture, called *Paschimatanāsana* in Sanskrit. This too belongs to the group of basic Yoga postures. It very closely resembles the Head-to-Knee Pose, except that here both legs are stretched out, instead of just one.

TECHNIQUE: Sit up straight, with both legs extended, feet together, hands on sides. Take a deep breath, hold it a few seconds while slightly raising the upper part of your body, then begin to exhale, at the same time slowly bending forward until your hands grasp your big toes—or the soles of your feet—and your head touches your knees. Do not bend the knees, which should remain straight.

Remain in this position, holding the breath for a few seconds, then release your grip and return to the sitting position again.

Repeat once more and relax.

TIME: Hold the posture from two to fifteen seconds. Do it twice at first. If you wish, you may increase the number up to six times by adding one turn every fourteen days.

BENEFITS: The benefits of the Stretching Posture are much the same as those of the Head-to-Knee Pose. It helps overcome constipation, indigestion, lumbago, and to reduce abdominal fat. It massages the pelvic region, gives an invigorating pull to the hamstring muscles and the sciatic nerves. Sluggish bowels become more active through the practice of this Asana. It is also practiced in advanced stages of Yoga for its spiritual values.

CAUTION: When releasing the Stretching Posture to return to the original sitting position, do it slowly and smoothly,

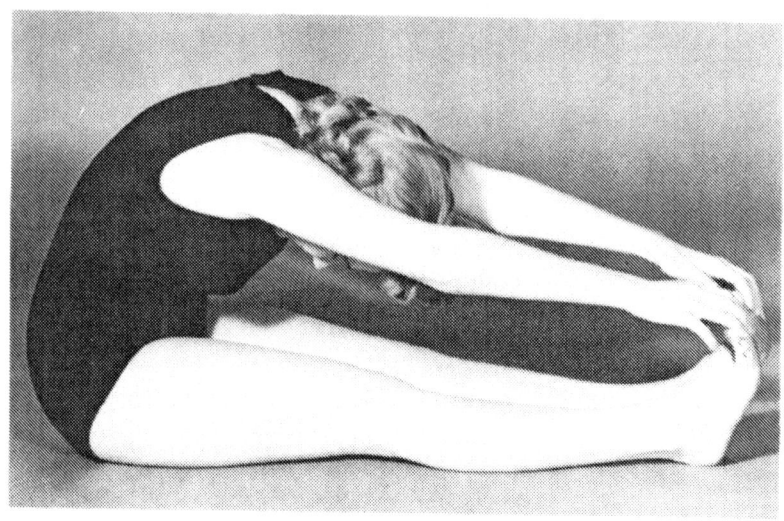

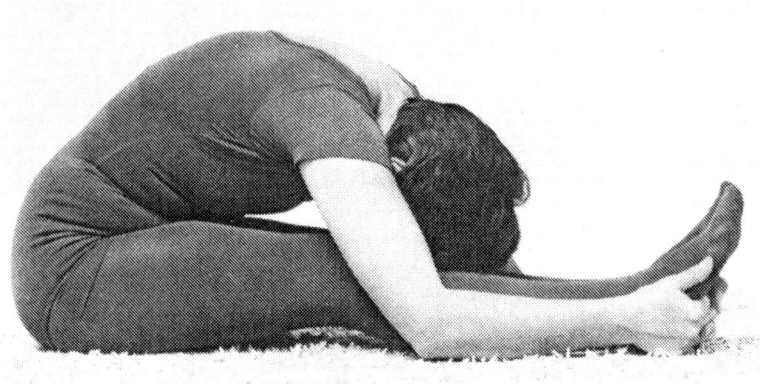

The Stretching Posture, or *Paschimatanāsana,* helps the digestion, reduces abdominal fat, and invigorates the pelvic region. It also benefits the sciatic nerves and helps prevent lumbago.
(Top photo by Miller)

never in one sudden, jerking, upward movement. People suffering from constipation should practice it especially carefully. If at first you cannot reach your feet with your hands, you may

Third Week

grasp your ankles or calves instead; or try using a belt, handkerchief or towel for a strap, as in the Head-to-Knee posture. Be sure not to bend the knees.

Now lie down and take a brief rest.

The Plough Posture

Next you will do still another of the basic Yoga postures, the Plough. It is called *Halāsana* in Sanskrit.

TECHNIQUE: First assume the Reverse Posture, whether with or without the aid of the table. Then slowly, without bending the knees, start to lower both legs *while exhaling*. When your toes reach the ground behind your head, you have achieved the Plough Posture.

The Plough Posture, or *Halāsana*, not only keeps the spine flexible but affects the thyroid gland, the liver, and the spleen.
(Photo by David Hernandez)

Place the palms on the floor and remain in this position for a while, trying to do deep breathing. This may be somewhat uncomfortable at first, but in a few days it will become easier for you. Then, while exhaling, return to the lying position, slowly lowering the spine until it again touches the floor, vertebra by vertebra. You accomplish this by bending the knees slightly, placing them above the forehead, then slowly gliding them down over the face, continuing a slow-motion unfoldment of the entire posture.

TIME: Retain the posture five seconds at first, then gradually increase to four minutes by adding five seconds per week. Repeat from two to four times, adding one time every fourteen days.

BENEFIT: The Plough Posture affects the thyroid gland, massages the liver and spleen, and stretches and pulls the vertebrae, thereby keeping the spine in a youthful, flexible, and healthy condition. People suffering from stiffness, obesity, muscular rheumatism, enlarged liver and spleen, constipation, indigestion, and arthritis will find this posture especially beneficial.

CAUTION: If you have not limbered up through previous exercise, do not attempt right away the final stage of this posture unless you have a naturally very flexible spine. Otherwise do not try to touch the floor with the toes for a few days. After that, try lying down with the head about two feet away from the wall—if you are tall the distance will have to be proportionately longer. Get into the Reverse Posture, then begin to lower the legs until the toes touch the wall; then start "walking" down the wall with the toes. Take care not to *force* them any lower than your spine comfortably allows, otherwise you are likely to injure a rigid muscle and the pain may last several weeks. This could only frighten you away from attempting the posture again, so please be very careful!

For a variation of the Plough Posture, bend both knees instead of keeping them straight—in this case the knees should almost touch the ears. The toes will be on the floor. After finishing the posture, lie down, relax, and then take a few deep breaths.

Third Week

The Camel Posture

So far you have been mostly doing postures which require a forward bend, and only one, The Cobra, which utilizes a backward bend. The Camel Posture, or *Ustrāsana* in Sanskrit, which you will do now is another backward-bending exercise.

TECHNIQUE: Kneel down, sit on the heels, keeping the toes outstretched, and place the hands on the floor, directly behind the toes. Lean on them. Throw the head back.

Now, while inhaling deeply, slowly raise the buttocks off the knees, lifting the lower part of the body and arching the spine.

Remain in this posture while holding the breath, then return to original position: sit down on the heels, move head forward and exhale. Take a rest and repeat the whole exercise.

TIME: Hold the posture for six seconds, gradually increasing

The Camel Posture, or *Ustrāsana*, has a good effect on the thyroid gland and the gonads. (Photo by Jim Buhr)

the time to thirty seconds. Repeat from two to five times. It is better to practice this posture in the morning than in the evening.

BENEFITS: The Camel Posture affects the thyroid glands and gonads, or sex glands. It gives elasticity to the spine and tones the muscles supporting it. People suffering from gas, constipation, displacement of the vertebrae and of the pelvic organs, that is, the ureter, urethra, urine bladder, uterus and Fallopian tubes, will find this exercise useful provided the displacement is not of a major nature.

CAUTION: People suffering from hernia should not attempt this posture.

The Lion Posture

Let us now do the Lion Posture, *Simhāsana* in Sanskrit. In spite of its fierce and grotesque appearance, this pose has no equal for overcoming various throat ailments, especially a sore throat.

One of my students, a woman lawyer, tells how with the help of this posture she once won a case she would otherwise have surely lost. On the morning of the trial she awoke with a bad sore throat. She felt desperate. Then, remembering the Lion Pose, she did it about six times in succession. It worked like magic—the throat cleared up completely. Incidentally, this Asana is exceptional in that it is effective within a few minutes.

TECHNIQUE: Sit down on your heels, or in a chair if sitting on the heels is difficult for you, and place your hands on your knees. After taking a deep breath, exhale and stick out your tongue as far as possible, almost to the point of gagging. While doing this, stiffen up the fingers and spread them far apart. Open the mouth and eyes wide, and tense the neck and throat as well as the entire body, but especially the throat. Keep this posture for a few seconds, remaining very tense, then relax.

Third Week

The Lion Posture, or *Simhāsana*, tones the muscles and ligaments of the throat. (Photo by Jim Buhr)

In the final stage you first cross your ankles and then sit down on the crossed heels.

TIME: This posture normally can be repeated two to three times, but if you are on the point of developing a sore throat, do it six to ten times in succession several times a day.

BENEFITS: The Lion Posture affects the throat by sending an extra supply of blood to it. The Lion Posture also massages and tones the muscles and ligaments of the throat, at the same time strengthening and invigorating the entire body. People suffering from enlarged tonsils and a throat susceptible to infection should practice this posture daily.

98   LESSON THREE

CAUTION: Do not do this posture immediately following a meal, as you are likely to throw up.

The Footlift Pose: Second Movement

We shall now attempt the second movement of the Footlift Pose or "Stork," the first part of which we did in Lesson Two; by now you are probably able to remain standing without hopping around on one leg like a lame bird.

TECHNIQUE: Get into the first movement of the posture, as

The Footlift Pose, Second Movement. Practiced persistently, this exercise will develop steadiness and balance. (Photo by Miller)

directed in Lesson One. Stand on the right foot, keeping the left foot high on the right thigh and holding it with the right hand. Keep the left knee on a level with the right knee. Now take a deep breath and, while exhaling it, bend forward until the fingers of your left hand touch the ground. Bend your head down to touch the knee, or try to do so. The left heel should press firmly against the abdomen. Remain in this position, holding the breath; then return to the first position, take a few deep breaths, and relax. Repeat the exercise again. Next do the same exercise standing on the left leg. Just as in the second breathing exercise of your first lesson, keep the buttocks *in* when bending forward. The bending should be done from *above* the waist, by the spine.

TIME: Hold this position from two to twenty seconds, repeating it two to five times.

BENEFITS: The Footlift strengthens the legs, massages the abdomen, and is a beneficial exercise for people troubled with constipation, gas, and fat around the abdomen. It is especially good for acquiring steadiness and balance.

The Cleansing Breath

To do the Cleansing Breath, stand straight with feet close together and arms hanging loosely at the sides. Take a deep breath, hold it for a little while, then purse your lips as if you were going to whistle. Now start exhaling forcefully, little by little, but do not blow the air out as if you were blowing out a candle, and do not puff out the cheeks which should, rather, be hollowed.

These successive and forceful exhalations will feel almost like slight coughs which expel the air until the lungs are completely empty. The effort of the exhalation should be felt in the chest and in the back.

Rest for a little while, then repeat. After a week you may repeat this routine several times a day.

BENEFITS: The Cleansing Breath, as its name indicates, cleans and ventilates the lungs; it also tones up the entire system. You should do the Cleansing Breath at the conclusion of each lesson, just before the final relaxation.

The Walking Breathing Exercise

Before concluding the lesson with relaxation we shall do the Walking Breathing exercise. This is done in exactly the same way as Rhythmic Breathing except that you do it while walking. Use each step as a count, as you used the pulse beat in Rhythmic Breathing.

Stand erect, exhale first, then start walking, right foot first. Take four steps while inhaling, hold the breath in for two steps, exhale for four steps, and hold the breath out for two steps. Without stopping, continue the routine: inhale on four steps, hold the breath in for two steps, and so forth. *Do not* interrupt the walking—keep it rhythmical. The breathing should be done in *one continuous flow:* do not inhale in four short breaths, a mistake which many beginners tend to make. Inhale *one deep breath* to the count of four, hold it to the count of two, exhale it to the count of four, and again hold the emptiness to the count of two. This completes one round. Make five such rounds a day the first week—no more—adding one round per week.

If you feel that four steps are too long for you, count three steps and hold one. If, on the contrary, four are not enough and you feel you want to continue the inhalation, take six steps or even eight, and hold the breath on a count of three or four steps respectively. In either case, you should take an even number of steps while breathing in and out, as the retention is done in half the time taken for inhalation or exhalation.

You can do the Walking Breathing exercise not only while going through your lesson, but also at any other time while you are walking, especially when the air is clean—in a park, a

Third Week

forest, or at the seashore. You can do it while walking to your car or bus, descending a staircase, on your way to pick up your mail from the letter box, during a coffee break in your office, in fact, whenever you think of it. Simply interrupt your usual walking tempo, stop to inhale and exhale deeply. Then start rhythmic breathing to the count of slow and even steps.

Conclude your lesson by doing the relaxation and meditation.

ON RELAXATION AND THE ENDOCRINE GLANDS

Before a new student joins my class, he is usually asked, among other things, what is his reason for taking up Yoga.

The great majority, I find, want to learn how to relax. Even if they have other motives, relaxation is almost invariably mentioned.

Men and women alike seem to suffer widely from what they call "nerves." One constantly hears people saying, "I am all on edge," "My nerves are in bad shape," "It's nothing but my poor nerves. . . ." Such neuro-muscular tensions are seldom due to disease of either the nerves or the muscles, but rather reactions of the body to the impressions of the mind. They stem from conscious or unconscious thoughts dictated mostly by various kinds of fears.

Take the case of Mr. Al D., for instance. This man came to me complaining of nervous tension. "It drives me simply crazy," were his exact words. "The point is that I am in the grip of this thing and can do nothing about it. Take yesterday morning, for instance. I got up feeling fine, relaxed as a kitten. Then came the mail, and the moment I saw those bills and the letter from my lawyer I felt my neck muscles tighten. I couldn't stop it—it spread to the upper part of my back and shoulders. Then I got a headache, and at the office I wasn't worth my salt. Last night I lay imagining all sorts of things, including the loss of my job, and today I feel like jumping into the lake. That tightening of the muscles seems to have no end. Isn't there some way a man can throw off this thing? Loosen up, relax, be himself again?"

It took quite a while to teach Mr. D. the deep breathing technique, for he kept doing it the hard—and consequently the wrong—way: He seemed unable to relax of his own accord. Finally I made him lie down, close his eyes and imagine him-

Third Week

self at the seashore, with the waves coming and receding, coming and receding, coming and receding. Then, kneeling behind him so that he could hear me breathe, I began doing Deep Breathing after instructing him to visualize a mounting wave with each inhalation and a receding one with each exhalation. "Let me do the deep breathing alone at first," I suggested. "You can join in whenever you are sufficiently relaxed to go along." Within a few minutes we were breathing in unison.

I have seldom witnessed such a wild outburst of joy as this man gave way to, following his first relaxation lesson. Once he discovered there was a way to *learn* to relax, he simply could not contain himself. In cases like his, the real trouble is that the tension itself sets up a vicious circle, with mental strain the result of purely physical conditions, or body tension the result of emotional stresses and strains. Once this is the case, the circle is difficult to break. For example, a thyroid that is overactive or exhausted as the result of hard living may in turn produce a physical state that leads to emotional disturbance; and this further accentuates "nervousness," or neuro-muscular tension. The more wound-up a person becomes, the more difficult it is for the body to shake itself free.

Generally speaking, with civilized people, the tensions *start* with their imaginative, fear-ridden responses to their overcomplicated environment. Man's effort to find a way out of this dilemma goes a long, long way back. He tries just about every remedy: alcohol, drugs, cigarettes, long walks, mowing the lawn or playing golf. He tries sex, war, and religion, and various "isms." He sometimes also tries death. But his problem is yet to be solved.

Right now he is trying to escape to the moon. He will probably succeed, too, but he will take his fears and tensions with him. Yet since man can neither run away from nor forget himself, wouldn't the most logical answer be to turn within, to his own inner self, and there seek—and find—the solution to his driving problem? Curiously enough, this is the one remedy he seldom thinks of trying, except in a few individual cases.

Some years ago a German magazine carried an article entitled, "The Death of the Manager: The Scourge of the Successful Man . . . Yoga to Remedy 'Manager-Disease' . . . Ancient India Prescription . . . Relaxation Instead of Tension . . . Daily Breathing Exercises Prolong Life."[1] An impressive illustration then pictured the manager lying dead at the entrance to the conference room. A snuffed-out candle in the background stood as a symbol of the premature end of his life, for it could have burned much longer. The silhouette of several Yoga postures below suggested that this was what the manager had failed to do. Otherwise he might have prolonged his life.

The article said that half the big executives, businessmen, politicians and other persons of importance who had recently died "in the prime of life" usually had succumbed to degenerative diseases such as weak hearts or circulatory disturbances. All these men had died of overwork, overstrain, overexhaustion, over-tension. Also they had eaten too much, drunk too much, and smoked too much. But their main trouble had been stress. Therefore diabetes, arthritis, coronary thrombosis, constipation, headaches, neurasthenia, a pot-belly and a sway back had been common ailments among them. Usually they had fought their troubles with pills and drugs which did not touch the real hidden enemies—fear, tension, and wrong concepts of living.

"The manager," this same article went on, "could have smoked cigars and sipped highballs for another thirty years, had he known about Hatha Yoga." After this statement a description of the breathing exercises and postures followed, urging everyone to learn from Yoga its invaluable technique

---

[1] *Muenchener Illustrierte,* September 12, 1953.

Third Week

for the relaxation of body and mind, for the preservation of youth and health, and for the prolongation of the span of life.

Except for the cigars and highballs, which to me are a strange kind of reward to hold out for taking up Yoga, the article was much to the point and very convincing. Furthermore, it probably aroused great interest in Yoga among those who read it. For why not learn the secrets of relaxation, youth, health and longevity from those who have proven through the centuries the effectiveness of their system, instead of relying on panaceas offered by people who themselves are engaged in a "rat-race"?

It is true that no mechanical device or gadget, no pill or nostrum, can be effective for very long when the problem is to relieve the mind from stress and the body from strain. And physical and mental relaxation is one of the ABCs of Yoga. You yourself may have noticed by now, if you have been doing the relaxation exercises regularly at the end of every lesson without skipping, how these exercises induce not only muscular, but also mental ease. This will become still more apparent as you practice the Headstand which we began today. Still another step toward true relaxation will come with the meditation which will be part of your final lesson.

Yet how can the Headstand relax one, you may ask, when on your first attempt, it has made you feel anything *but* relaxed? The answer is simply that you must not become impatient— it will not be long before you *will* feel at ease while standing upside down. There is, by the way, a good physical explanation for this, and I would like to take time right here to go into the physiology of what happens when the human body is upturned in this way.

The Headstand has an effect on two of the glands we have already described as the most vital ones in our body, the pituitary and the pineal, both of which are located in the head cavity. When you stand upside down, a larger amount of blood —blood which is being further enriched through deep breath-

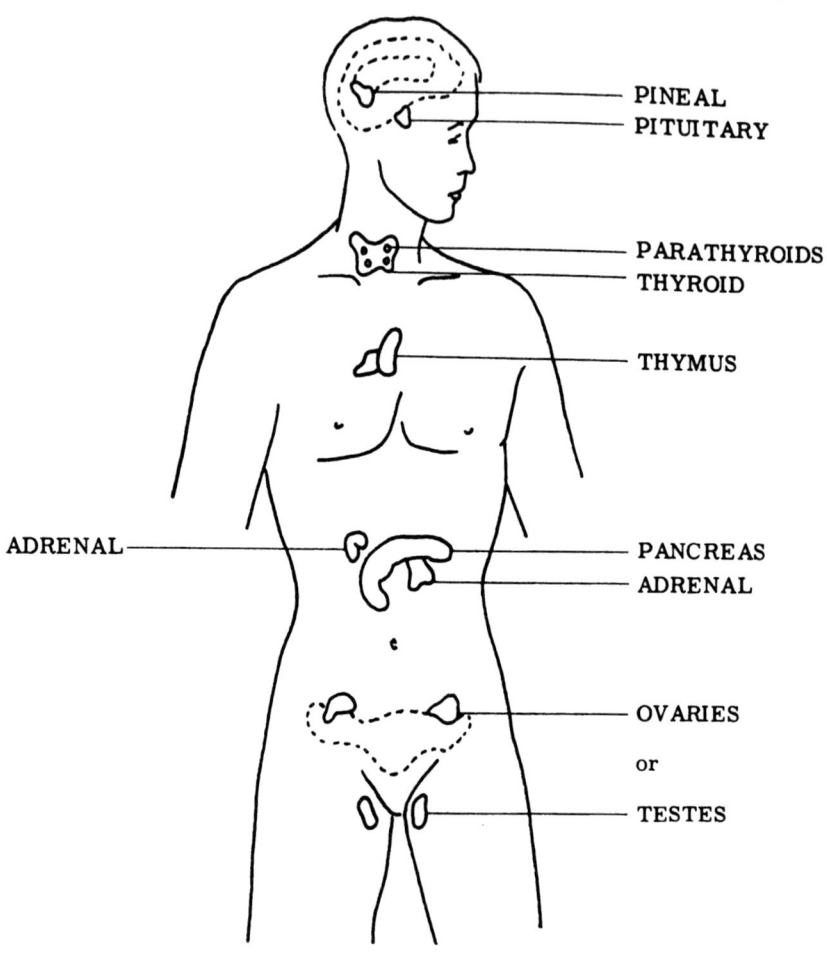

Chart of the Endocrine Gland System.

ing—begins to flow to the head, and thus carries an extra supply of energy to these glands.

You may remember from the chapter on the endocrine system in my previous book what are the functions of the various glands. If not, the chart on this page will help refresh your memory. As you see, the endocrines are all situated at strategic points in the body. In addition to the pituitary and pineal in

Third Week 107

the cranium, the thyroid and parathyroids are behind the larynx at the base of the neck; the thymus is in the upper part of the chest above the heart (this gland, incidentally, shrinks in size and importance as we stop growing); the two adrenals are on top of the kidneys; and the gonads, or sex glands, lie in the lower part of the trunk, below the digestive organs.

The functions of all of the endocrine, or ductless, glands are interconnected, although each has its own duties to perform. Another name for the endocrines is *glands of internal secretions,* because they secrete various hormones, without which our organism could not function properly. And hormones are best defined as those various substances formed inside the endocrine glands which activate specifically receptive organs. Insulin, for instance, is a hormone secreted by the thyroid gland, cortisone by the adrenal glands, and so on. If any of the endocrine glands becomes either over- or underactive, we may lose or accumulate weight in various parts of the body.

The master gland or, as it has often been referred to, the "boss of them all," is the pituitary, for it regulates the activities of all the others. Although very small in size—no larger than a green pea—the pituitary is nevertheless of paramount importance to our well being. As many as twelve various hormones are known to be manufactured inside it.

"We know for example," writes Dr. John A. Schindler in his stimulating book, *How to Live 365 Days a Year,*[2] "that there is one hormone of the pituitary that raises blood pressure, another that makes smooth muscles contract, one that inhibits the kidneys from producing urine, one that stimulates the kidneys to make more urine. Then there is a whole group of hormones that regulate the other endocrine glands of the body. These other glands produce many more hormones to regulate just everything that goes on in our bodies."

---

[2] Englewood Cliffs, N.J.: Prentice-Hall, Inc., 1954.

The reason I am including all this information in this discussion is that out of it you may evolve a real understanding of many of your own health problems. Think of the human body as potentially threatened by an enemy army, whether in the form of bacterial invasion, virus infection, or emotional stress. The after-effects of drugs, injuries, operations, exposure to high altitude, to excessive heat, cold, moisture or dryness, muscular over-exertion, shock, and even starvation are included among these dangers. Think of the pituitary gland as a master spirit which is able, alone, to fight off any attack by any of these enemies, and you will begin to get the picture.

More specifically, the various dangers threatening our well-being are sometimes referred to as *stressors,* while the result of their negative influence is called *stress.* This, at any rate, is the way Dr. Hans Selye described them in his monumental work, *Stress of Life,*[3] and in *The Story of the Adaptation Syndrome.*[4] He explains that the most dangerous and most powerful of all stressors are those of our own emotions that upset and aggravate us. That is why the job of an executive often carries with it diabetes or peptic ulcers: it is the result of driving one's self into performing all kinds of unpleasant duties, the duties of a hard taskmaster. A man in a subordinate job, on the other hand, is more likely to suffer from colds, tiredness, nausea, weakness, arthritis, asthma, inflammation and all sorts of aches and pains. This is, of course, a generalization; ulcers or arthritis may happen to anyone.

The findings of Dr. Hans Selye have thrown a completely new light on the function of the pituitary gland and its capacity to mobilize the body's defense forces against *any* kind of invaders.

It is impossible here to go into further details of this fascinating subject, as it requires more time and space than I have

---

[3] New York: McGraw-Hill Book Company, Inc., 1956.
[4] Montreal, Canada: Acta, Inc., 1952.

Third Week

at my disposal. But I would like to alert you to the fact that most of our diseases are *not* due to the toxins of virus or bacteria as such, but to the stressors that, offsetting the normal activity of the pituitary gland, throw it off balance, and thus lower our resistance to illness.

Because the worst offenders are the psychic stressors which produce emotional upsets, a high-strung, intellectual person is more subject to them than a less sensitive individual. And, what we often blame on our nerves should actually be blamed on our glands.

Here is a secret of relaxation and youth given by a man·who doesn't know what tension and stress are and who at ninety-four, looks, feels and works like a person half his age. "My strength lies in never hating or even opposing anyone," Jacques Romano told the writer interviewing him. Then he went on to explain that he was a Buddhist when with a Buddhist, a Christian when with a Christian, a dog when with a dog, etc. In conclusion he said: "Treat people as if they were flowers and you will have a happy life." [5]

You probably see for yourself now where Yoga comes into the picture: The practice of the Headstand has a direct influence on the functions of the pituitary gland which regulates our entire well-being.

Rhythmic breathing and relaxation exercises enable us to overcome muscular tension and mental strain which also adversely affect the hormonal secretion of this gland.

Thus you can see how Yoga can restore the normal working order of our entire organism, and why relaxation of body and mind go hand in hand with health, youth, happiness and a long life.

---

[5] *The New Yorker,* July 19, 1958.

Lesson Four

FOURTH WEEK

Physical pain, melancholy, unsteady limbs, irregular inhalation and exhalation, all are causing distraction of the mind.
—YOGA DARSHANA

TODAY YOU ARE STARTING THE SECOND HALF OF THE COURSE AND only three more weeks remain before you will have completed it.

So far, you have learned seven of the basic exercises, ten additional postures, and six breathing exercises. Choose from among them those which best suit your particular physical condition as well as your personal needs, ability and time. From now on, use these as the basis for your own exercise routine. Stay with the basic postures and vary only the additional ones. On the first day of each new week's lesson, however, you may, if you wish, give preference to the new postures, in order to get acquainted with them.

Even after you have completed the course, it is advisable for you to re-read the instructions from time to time, directly before assuming one or another of the postures, since there is always a tendency to start deviating from the correct way of doing the exercises without being at all aware of it. This, then, will be a way to keep a check on yourself.

I remember once watching a former student doing the postures together with his wife and children. The four of them went through the exercises at such high speed, keeping time in unison besides, that it looked to me more like an acrobatic performance than a Yoga lesson. For without poise, concentration, relaxation, and, above all, without deep breathing, these postures, no matter how well executed, automatically cease to be Yoga Asanas and become ordinary calisthenics. This is the sort of mistake that checking will help you avoid.

Yoga postures should remain an individual matter regardless of the number of pupils doing them together.

Today, after you have finished the Rocking exercise, we shall start our lesson with the Headstand and do it against the wall—but only if you feel absolutely sure that you are ready to "graduate" from the corner. Otherwise continue as before, using the corner as a safety measure until you no longer need it.

The Headstand: Second Stage

TECHNIQUE: To do the Headstand against the wall, keep the pad about a foot away from the wall. Then kneel down in front of it, interlock your fingers, and place the hands on the pad. The distance between the hands and the wall should be approximately that of the length of your arms from wrist to elbow.

Place your head, about one inch above the forehead, on the mat and, nesting it in the hollow of the palms, find a comfortable position for it. When standing on your head, always remember to lean on the forearms for better support: hence the elbows should not be kept too far apart. Now move your feet closer toward your head, take a deep breath and, lowering

Fourth Week

the buttocks, make a slight jumping movement in order to get your feet off the floor.

Continue to raise your legs, with knees bent, in a slow-motion movement. When you get half way up, tuck in your buttocks and only then straighten the knees; otherwise you are bound to lose your balance and fall over. To avoid this, quickly bend the knees and prop up the soles of the feet against the wall.

Until the Headstand has been perfected, it is helpful to place the feet against the wall for balance. (Photo by Jim Buhr)

Hold this position for a while—the body in a straight line from head to knees, knees bent, feet on the wall for support. Now, keeping your feet together, close your eyes, and do some deep breathing.

After a while, straighten your knees and try to get your feet away from the wall. Hold this position for about thirty seconds, then bend the knees and start lowering your legs slowly until the toes touch the floor. Don't forget to keep the toes inverted so as not to injure them. It is important to come down slowly, otherwise you may fall on your knees and hurt yourself.

Should you begin losing your balance while standing on your head, quickly put your feet against the wall. But do not remain like this—leaning against the wall with out-stretched legs—as this is bound to result in arching the spine and offsetting the correct posture of the Headstand. Keep knees bent.

Now get up, raise your arms, take a deep breath, then lie down for a rest.

TIME: Increase the duration of the Headstand by fifteen seconds a week. The maximum time is twelve minutes, when done along with other exercises.

The Swan Posture

Next you will do an exercise which, as one says in English, kills two birds with one stone. This posture is called *Swan-āsana* in Sanskrit. The first movement affects the spine, shoulders, pelvic region and wrists, while the second benefits the digestive organs, the abdomen and the knees. The starting position is the same as in the Cobra Pose.

TECHNIQUE: Lie down on the abdomen, palms on the floor at shoulder level, elbows up, toes inverted. Inhale deeply and, leaning on the palms, raise your head, shoulders, chest and abdomen off the floor until you have straightened the elbows.

As I just mentioned, this posture resembles the Cobra Pose, with the difference that here the elbows are kept straight and

The Swan Posture, or *Swandāsana*: (*Above*) The first movement affects the spine, shoulders, pelvic region and wrists. (*Below*) The second movement helps to keep the digestive organs, the abdomen, and the knees in good shape. (Photos by Jim Buhr)

the toes inverted. Remain in this position for as long as you can. Hold your breath, then exhale while getting into a kneeling position. Do not move the palms, which should remain flat on the floor. Now your thighs are pressed against the abdomen, your forehead touches the ground and your buttocks rest on your heels.

Stay in this position for a while, holding your breath. Then, while inhaling, raise your buttocks off your heels and move the body forward (again without changing the position of your palms) until you have returned to the previous Cobra-like position. Having accomplished this, remain in this posture, holding your breath; then, as you exhale, move back into the kneeling posture again.

TIME: Repeat this to-and-fro movement three to four times, making sure you do the breathing correctly.

BENEFITS: This exercise strengthens the spine, arms, wrist, chest and throat. It also straightens the back and shoulders. In the kneeling position the thighs massage the abdomen by pressing against it and the shoulders and arms receive a good pull. The to-and-fro movements help promote better elimination and reduce the abdomen.

The Twist Posture: First Movement

Take a little rest before starting the first movement of the Twist Posture. It is called *Ardha Matsyendrāsana* in Sanskrit, quite a tongue-twister for most non-Indians, and also quite a spinal twist for everyone. We shall take it in three stages so that it should not be difficult for you to learn.

The Twist also belongs to the group of basic Yoga postures.

TECHNIQUE: Sit up straight with both legs outstretched. Cross your right foot over your left knee, place it firmly on the floor, keeping the left hand on the right toes. Stretch out the right arm and twist it around the back of your waist line as far as you can. The open palm and the wrist should be resting on the left hip bone. Keep both head and spine straight, and the *entire* sole of your right foot on the floor. Inhale deeply. While exhaling, slowly start turning your head, then shoulders and back, to the right. When you have finished exhaling, you will find that you are able to twist still a little more to the right. Do not bend your head while doing so: keep your chin *up*.

Fourth Week 117

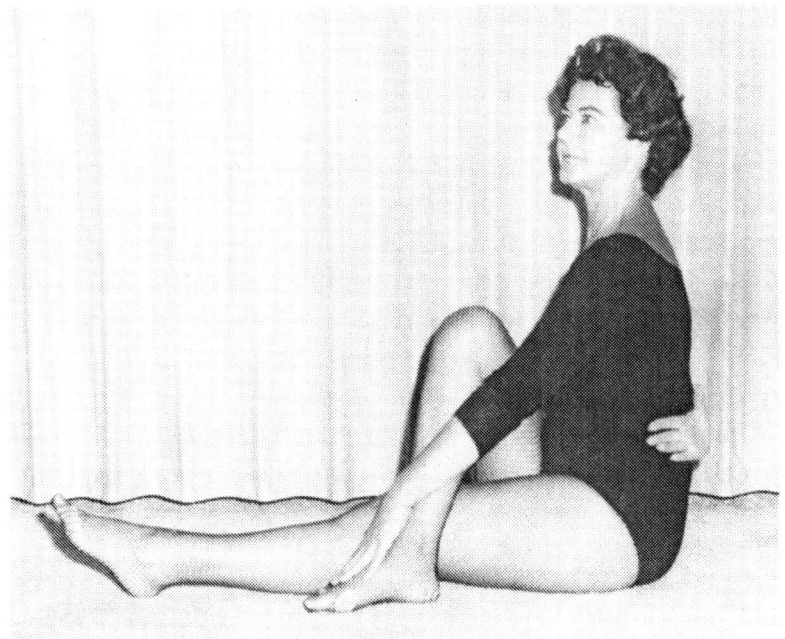

The Twist Posture, or *Ardha Matsyendrāsana*, is one of the basic Yoga poses. Done in three stages, it should not be too difficult to learn. (Photo by Jim Buhr)

Remain in this position, holding your breath for as long as you can, then start exhaling, at the same time slowly unwinding the twist until the head, shoulders and back are in the original position again. Pause for a while and repeat the Twist. Then reverse the position of legs and hands, and assume the same position with the twist to the left side.

TIME: Maintain this posture for five seconds, holding your breath. Increase the time to one minute, adding five seconds per week. When holding it for more than several seconds, resume the deep breathing while remaining in the posture, but always unwind on exhalation. Repeat the twist two to three times.

BENEFITS: The Twist affects the adrenal glands. It also tones up sluggish kidneys and a congested liver and spleen. Obesity, constipation, and indigestion are counteracted by the practice of this posture. The spine and its deep muscles are strengthened and made flexible; stooping shoulders, a bent back, and defective posture are corrected. People suffering from asthma should emphasize this posture as well as the Shoulderstand, the Headstand, and the Supine Posture.

The Twist, especially the last stage of it, is a beautiful posture. When you begin to do the slow turning of the body to either side, you should feel like a peacock majestically unfolding his large, colorful fan.

After finishing the exercise, lie down and rest until your breathing becomes normal again; then breathe deeply several times.

The Abdominal Lift

Now get up to do the Abdominal Lift, called *Uddyiana Bandha* in Sanskrit. It is considered one of the very essential Yoga exercises and is practiced not only for its physical values but for the way it also influences our psychic development. This last is true even though this pose does not make either a particularly aesthetic or impressive picture.

TECHNIQUE: Stand with feet about a foot apart, inhale deeply, exhale *with force*. Then, *without inhaling again*, draw in the abdominal muscles with a strong upward pull, until a hollow forms under the ribs. Place your hands on your thighs, bend the knees a little, and slightly tip your trunk forward *without lowering it*. The diaphragm then rises easily. Keep both hands pressed firmly against the thighs when leaning on them. Stay in this position as long as you can without breathing. Relax. Stand up straight and resume normal breathing. Repeat the Abdominal Lift only once more.

TIME: This exercise should not be done more than twice in

Fourth Week 119

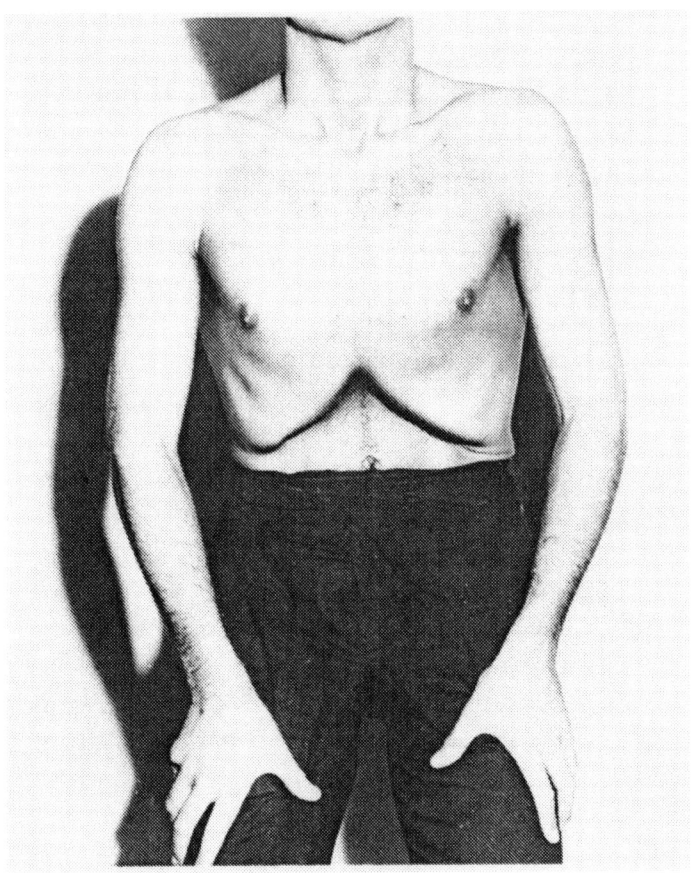

The Abdominal Lift, or *Uddyiana Bandha,* is practiced by the yogis for both spiritual and physical benefits. (Photo by Jim Buhr)

the first few days. You can gradually bring it up to seven times, adding one time per week.

BENEFITS: The Uddyiana Bandha strengthens the abdominal muscles and flabby stomach; it brings relief from gas, constipation, indigestion and liver trouble. Yogis also practice this exercise to develop spiritual force. It is considered to be the best exercise for toning up those nerves which have their roots in the solar plexus region.

The Abdominal Lift is also often used by the yogis for internal cleansing. For this, take several glasses of water, always at room temperature, with about a quarter of a teaspoon of salt per glass, and then do the contracting and relaxing movement several times in standing, sitting and lying position.

Just as a matter of interest I must mention here that one of my students recently sent me a booklet on the "avalanche treatment,"[1] which is based on cleansing the intestine by drinking large quantities of salt water and afterwards assuming five different positions in each of which successive contraction and relaxation of the abdomen is practiced. This is just another example of how, whether knowingly or not, Yoga methods infiltrate into Western health practices.

CAUTION: The Abdominal Lift should not be attempted by people suffering from a weak heart or serious abdominal or circulatory troubles.

To be able to check on whether the abdomen is being pulled in properly, do this exercise over a mirror placed against the back of a chair or sofa. Tip the mirror a little, otherwise you will not be able to see much, since your trunk must bend slightly forward. Be careful not to bend your knees too much, however, as the body *should not be lowered,* but should merely be slightly inclined.

A variation of this Bandha may be even easier for you to start with. Instead of keeping your abdomen drawn in, pull in and let go, pull in again and let go again. Repeat this two or three times more in quick successive movements. Relax and stand up straight. Repeat again and make sure that after the pulling-in movement, which should be done with full strength, you do not use any force at all for the pushing-out movement:

---

[1] Dr. Charles B. McFerrin, *The High Enema Without Apparatus,* New York: Benedict Lust Publications.

let this be gentle. In other words, the accent is on the sucking-in movement, not on the letting-go.

On the third day of your lesson you can do this quick contracting-and-relaxing exercise first, then follow with the full Abdominal Lift, which you should keep up for as long as you can without breathing.

The Churning Pose

The Churning Pose, called *Nauli* in Sanskrit, should not be attempted until after you have gained full mastery of the Stomach Lift.

TECHNIQUE: Assume the Stomach Lift, as described above. While still holding the exhalation, try to isolate the recti muscles by pushing forward with an effort and a contraction which is similar to that used when one feels constipated, the difference being that the "push" should be directed to either right, left or middle rectus in order to isolate it. If you have succeeded in isolating the middle rectus, it will stand out like a rigid vertical band, because in this area above the pubic bone the recti muscles alone can be separated. Having separated the middle rectus, proceed in similar manner to separate the right, then the left rectus. When isolating the right rectus, slightly incline the body to the right; when working on the left rectus, incline to the left. To make it easier for yourself, use a mirror placed on a chair, as recommended for doing the Stomach Lift. When you have succeeded in isolating each in turn, begin to "churn" these three muscles from left to right or from right to left, whichever is easier for you.

It is not easy to obtain results at once in this exercise, and one has to be patient. Often people push out the whole abdomen or do not perform the contraction properly. If you find yourself doing either, you can avoid mistakes by relaxing the muscles immediately and starting over again. Keep trying until

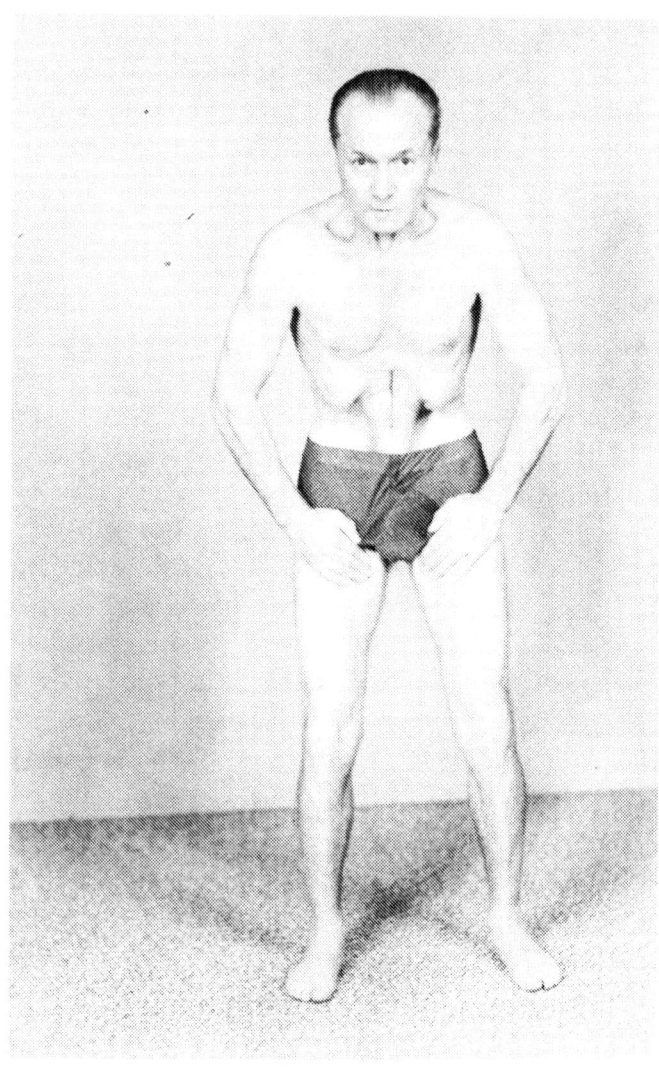

The Churning Pose, or *Nauli*, tones the abdominal region and keeps it healthy. (Photo by Fine Arts Studio, Chicago)

Fourth Week 123

you succeed in separating the recti muscles alone. Do not overtire yourself by making too many attempts at one time.

BENEFITS: The Nauli Pose tones up the abdominal region and keeps it healthy. It is also a good exercise for people troubled by indigestion, constipation or malfunction of the liver, spleen, kidneys, and pancreas. It helps as well to overcome ovarian insufficiency and painful periods.

CAUTION: People over forty-five should not start on the Nauli exercise without consulting an expert. The same applies to sufferers from appendicitis, tuberculosis of the abdomen or high blood pressure. Children should never do this exercise before the age of puberty.

The Footlift Pose: Third Movement

TECHNIQUE: Stand erect, place your right foot high up on your left thigh, holding it up with your left hand while putting your right arm around the back of your waistline, as you have done in the twist. Now with your right hand catch the toes of your right foot while letting go with the left hand. Take a deep breath, then, as you exhale; bend forward, until you touch the ground with your left hand and if possible your left knee with your forehead.

The third and final stage of the Footlift Pose may present some difficulties at first. Therefore it is meant only for more advanced students.

TIME: Maintain this posture for a few seconds, then return to the original standing position. Reverse position of your hands and feet and repeat the Footlift or "Stork" standing on your right foot.

BREATHING EXERCISES

First Breathing Exercise

Stand erect, feet together, hands along your sides. Inhale a

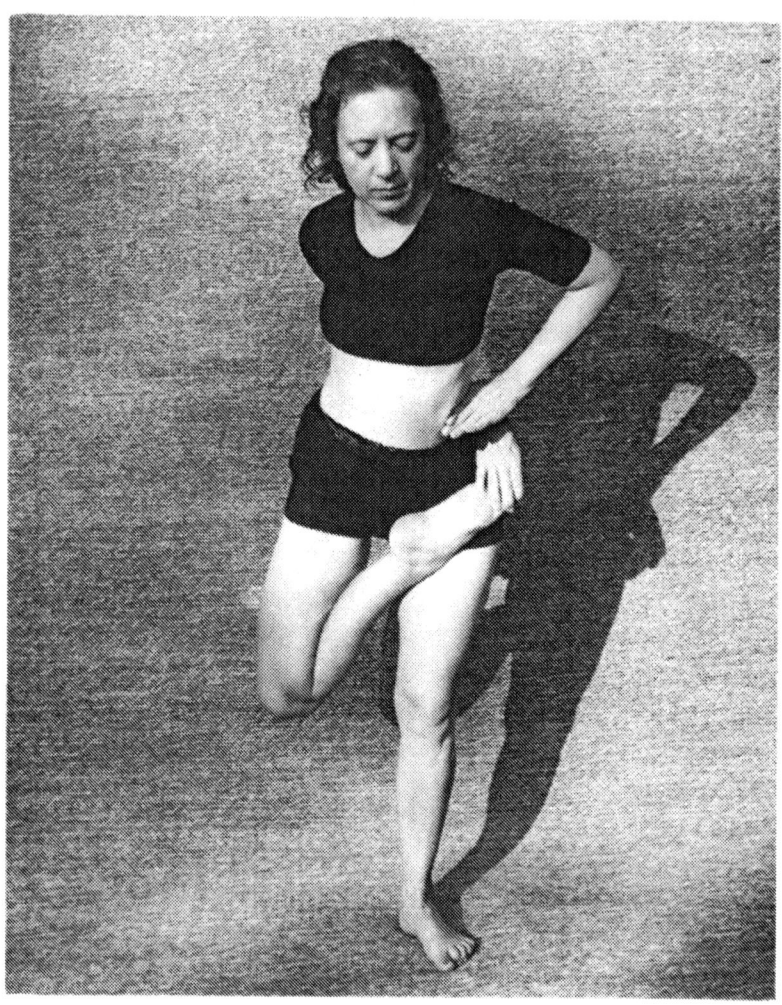

The Footlift Pose, in its third and final movement, requires the balance which only patient practice will give. (Photo by David Hernandez)

deep breath while slowly raising your heels off the floor until you are standing on your toes. Remain in this position for a few seconds, holding your breath. Exhale while slowly lowering your heels to the floor. Repeat two or three times.

Fourth Week

First Breathing Exercise, done while up on the toes, strengthens ankles, calves and weak arches. (Photo by Jim Buhr)

Now do the same, getting up on the toes of your right foot while keeping your left foot "hooked" to the back of your right leg just above the ankles.

TIME: Do this exercise two or three times, then repeat after reversing legs.

BENEFITS: Through the practice of this exercise you will be able to acquire good balance. It also strengthens your ankles and develops your calves. It is a good exercise for fallen arches and flabby calves.

Second Breathing Exercise

Stand erect, feet together, hands along sides. Inhale deeply while raising your arms (keeping the elbows straight) high above your head until your palms join each other. Stay in this position while holding your breath for a few seconds, then turn palms over so that the back of your hands are touching, and start slowly exhaling while lowering the outstretched arms. If you do this exercise correctly, you will experience a tingling sensation in your palms and fingers.

As you hold your breath while your palms are joined above your head, you should lock your throat by tightening its muscles to make sure that no breath escapes.

Repeat this breathing exercise again after a little pause, then finish with the Cleansing Breath.

Do not forget the Relaxation at the end of the lesson.

Fourth Week

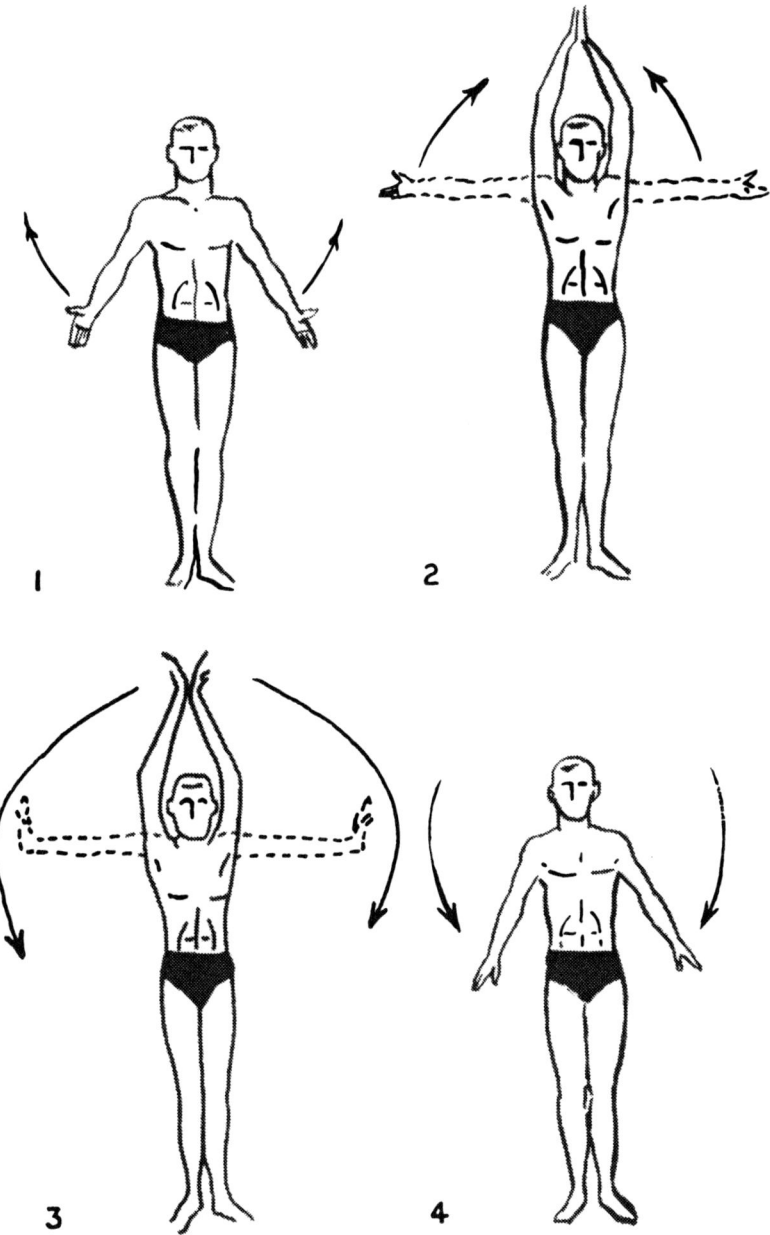

The final Breathing Exercise just before the Relaxation Period.

ON THE KUNDALINI POWER

> *Man can send a current only along a wire, but nature needs no wires to send her tremendous energies.*
>
> —Swami Vivekananda

The subject of our discussion today is the most secret and sacred of all Yoga practices, the awakening of the mysterious *Kundalini* (pronounced Koun-da-lee-nee), or Serpent power.

This belongs to the very advanced stages of Yoga, and it would be both impossible and dangerous to attempt to accomplish it here in America. Certainly it cannot be done by means of written instructions alone as each step requires the close supervision of one's *guru,* or spiritual guide.

But as a student of Yoga you should at least have some theoretical knowledge of Kundalini since its awakening is the heart and root of Yoga.

You may recall that at the end of our first lesson I mentioned *Prana,* explaining that this is an energy which exists in fluidic form in the atmosphere—and is present in everything that lives, from amoeba to man. The air, the sunshine, water, plants, minerals, food, all are impregnated with this life-substance which is the source of all energy, vitality, and power.

The yogis teach that Prana circulates in our bodies through a network of special channels which they have named *nadis,* from the word "nad," meaning movement in Sanskrit. The nadis are distributed throughout our astral body, just as the arteries, veins and nerves run through the physical body.[2]

---

[2] The astral body of a man is supposedly of the same shape and size as his physical body, but being of a finer substance, it is not visible, except to a clairvoyant. The yogis ascertain that we possess seven bodies including our gross physical body. The same conclusion was reached by three Frenchmen, Col. Albert Rochat, his pupil Charles Lancelin, and Dr. Gaston Durville, who have

Fourth Week

Being astral and not physical matter, the nadis are not visible to an ordinary eye: to perceive them requires a certain amount of clairvoyance. It was the ancient yogis' clairvoyant capacities that made their research work and findings possible: otherwise how could they have made such accurate studies of the human organism with all of its functions thousands of years before there were any instruments available? Clearly they must have known about the existence of the endocrine glands, since most of the Yoga postures were devised in order to affect one or several of these glands. Modern science, on the other hand, knew next to nothing about them until 1899 when endocrinology was officially born.

Yet Western scientists took, and continue to take, a very skeptical attitude toward the whole Yoga theory of Prana, for they can find no instruments which register it. Hence the entire subject is dismissed as non-existent.

Incidentally, the existence of Prana was known not only to the yogis of India, but also to the ancient occult schools of the Egyptians, the Hebrews, the Tibetans, the Chinese—later the Japanese—and finally the Greeks. Even the early Christians knew of this mysterious cosmic energy, for which there were many different names.

In the book of Genesis, for instance, the Hebrews called it *Neshemet Ruach Hayim,* which means Breath and Spirit of Life. The Tibetan *Naldjorpas* and the Japanese Zen school, which originated in China where it was brought by the Hindu missionaries, included Pranayama, the Yoga breath control exercises, in some of their practices; it was designed to raise the degree of circulation of Prana in the body. To keep the nadis clean, the yogis have devised special purification processes called Shodana.

---

been conducting extensive experiments and research for a number of years. (1. *L'Extériorisation de la Sensibilité,* par Albert Rochas: Editeur P. G. Leymarie, Paris. 2. *Méthode de Dédoublement Personnel,* par Charles Lancelin, Editeur Jean Meyer, Paris. 3. *Le Sommeil Magnétique,* par Gaston Durville, Paris.)

The three most important nadis are the *Shushumna*, the *Ida* (pronounced Eeda), and the *Pingala*. *Shushumna* is the chief nadi, located inside the spinal cord, with *Ida* and *Pingala* spiralling on either side like the two snakes in the Caduceus of Mercury.

Shushumna is represented by the straight rod; Ida and Pingala by the intercircling snakes, and the two petals of the *Ajna chakra* by a pair of wings. The small ball on top of the rod supposedly symbolizes the pineal gland.

Ida, flowing through the left nostril, is lunar, feminine, and cooling; Pingala, flowing through the right, is solar, masculine, and heating.

The physical counterparts of Ida and Pingala are probably the sympathetic chains of our nervous system, while that of Shushumna is the spinal cord. Taking root in the lowest center of Cosmic Energy, the *Muladhara chakra* (or wheel, as we explain below) extends to the highest center situated in the top of the head, the *Sahasrara chakra*.

Before we go any further, I suggest that you first look at the chakra chart on page 131 to get a clearer understanding of this subject.

In the picture you can see the seven major centers of Cosmic Energy situated on the spinal cord, or Shushumna nadi, and intercircled by the other two nadis, Ida and Pingala. These centers are called *chakras*, wheels, or *padmas*, lotuses. They are the astral counterparts of the plexuses of our anatomy. However, they should not be identified with them because, just like the nadis, the chakras also belong to another dimension.

There are seven basically significant chakras. The lowest, *Muladhara* chakra, is situated at the base of the spine. It controls the process of elimination and corresponds to the sacral plexus. This is the real occult center of the body because it encloses the secret, dormant energy called Kundalini which is symbolized by a snake coiled three and a half times with its

A chart of the *chakras*, which are the astral counterparts of our anatomic plexuses.

tail in its mouth. It closes the entrance to the chief nadi, Shushumna, which takes its root in the Muladhara chakra. Incidentally, all of Asia, as well as ancient Egypt and Greece, frequently represents Divine energy in the form of a snake.

The second is the *Svadishthana* chakra, situated opposite the genital organs. It controls sexual desires and corresponds to the epigastric plexus.

Third comes the *Manipura* chakra, which is opposite the navel and is concerned with digestive functions. Its counterpart is the solar plexus.

The fourth, or *Anahat* chakra, is at the level of the heart. It controls respiration and corresponds to the cardiac plexus.

The fifth, the *Visuddha* chakra, behind the throat, controls speech and corresponds to the pharyngeal plexus.

The sixth, *Ajna* chakra, is located between the eyebrows. It controls the autonomous nervous system and corresponds to the cavernous plexus, or more probably the pineal gland. It is the seat of the mystical "third eye" of Shiva, the seat of clairvoyance, according to the yogis. The biblical Yehovah is also often represented as having it. The Ajna chakra is where Shushumna, Ida, and Pingala meet and form the sacred knot called *Triveni*.

The seventh and last chakra is the *Sahasrara,* corresponding to the cortical layer in the brain. It is also known as the Thousand-Petalled Lotus.

All the lotuses, or chakras, have a certain number of petals, ranging from two to sixteen, with the highest chakra represented as having a great many petals.

When the Kundalini power, awakened by special exercises, passes from the lowest chakra, the Muladhara, through the central nadi, Shushumna, and through all the others, they begin to "spin" like true wheels and open their petals like lotuses. When Kundalini finally enters the last and highest center, the Sahasrara chakra, the yogi reaches his goal: "The divine marriage of Spirit and Matter" takes place. At this point, his individual consciousness unites with Universal Consciousness, and he enters a state of ultimate bliss, called *Samadhi*. It must be noted that even among yogis there are very few who attain a complete state of spiritual illumination.

Great mystics and saints of all religions have also on occa-

Fourth Week

sion experienced and described this state, but without possessing the knowledge of how to reach it consciously.

The ascending of the awakened Kundalini power, achieved by various practices and exercises, is the most secret of all Yoga teachings and is always given verbally by master to pupil. It cannot and should not ever be described.

In his *Higher Psychical Development*, Hereward Carrington [3] says that much has been done in order to prove that the mystical "Tree of Life" mentioned in the book of Genesis is connected with Kundalini. This extraordinary energy which brings with it the knowledge of good and evil was wrongly awakened by a being known in the Bible as Adam. The author suggests that the entire Genesis legend of the serpent is, according to Oriental views, merely a way of symbolizing the awakening of the fire serpent Kundalini, which is also the primordial electrical energy known as *Speirema* or the serpent coil. In the sacred writings of India this power is spoken of as coiled like a "slumbering serpent." In the book of Genesis it is symbolized as "The Serpent, more subtle than any beast of the field which the Lord has made." Eve, when this force stirred within her, was tempted to misuse it. Directed downward to the lower physical centers, the serpent force brings knowledge of evil; directed upward to the brain, it brings knowledge of good. Hence the dual operating of the solar force that is symbolized as the "Tree of Knowledge of Good and Evil." This fundamental key energy in our bodies is closely connected with fundamental sex energy and may be controlled and transmuted by certain Yoga practices.

As to the subject of sex itself: Like so many others, you may possibly be under the misapprehension that Yoga advocates the suppression of sex, since most of the yogis are ascetics. Let me

---

[3] New York: Dodd, Mead & Co., 1920.

say here that this is not so. The yogis merely know the secret of transmuting sex energy into more subtle forces, called *ojas*, and directing these into psychic channels. Through this transmutation, excess sex energy is neither lost nor suppressed: it is merely changed into finer substances, just as ice may be changed into water, or water into steam.

Suppression of sex usually results in all kinds of mental and physical troubles, in abnormalities or perversions. On the other hand, this same energy, instead of being utilized in the normal manner or else in healthful exercise and mental activity, may be drawn upward to the solar plexus or to the brain. This is a Yoga practice. When describing it in the chapter on sex in my previous book, I only very briefly mentioned that sex energy was closely connected with the Kundalini power, but did not touch upon its actual operation. Let us now take a closer look at it.

When awakened in a yogi, this solar energy gives him poise, harmony, freedom from desire and a lasting feeling of happiness. He then arrives at the realization of the true Self. The divine spark in him grows into a flame and merges into the Universal Consciousness. This God-realization is the final goal of all yogis. It is the highest state at which a human being may arrive on this earth.

Many need a lifetime, or several lifetimes to achieve this state, others only a few years. It also may come suddenly, like an unexpected gift. This has been known to happen not alone to yogis and rishis of India, but to mystics, saints and spiritually-developed persons the world over.

We ordinary human beings cannot expect to reach this exalted state of consciousness so long as we lead a worldly life and are caught up in the web of its illusions. But it is good to know that a paradise-like state *can* exist even on earth, that it is a reality, and that eventually, in other lives to come, we too may enter this realm of eternal bliss and untold happiness.

Fourth Week

To quote from *Yoga* by Major General Fuller,[4] "The Yoga philosophy has been the solace of millions for many centuries, not only in India but throughout the world. This philosophy has produced the greatest and most influential masters, Gautama, Christ, Mohammed, whose mastery over the Unknowable has been the driving force of nations. All these men were yogis of one sort or another. Their lives, though outwardly differing from one another were inwardly the same, and so was their teaching, which, in each case, led the aspirant to the one Reality, the Peace which passeth understanding."

---

[4] Philadelphia: David McKay Co., 1925.

Lesson Five

FIFTH WEEK

> *The numerable forms of philosophy, of arguments and of the rules capture the intellect in their nets and lead it away from the true knowledge.*
> —YOGABIJA UPANISHAD

The Headstand: Third Stage

We shall begin this week's lesson by doing the final stage of the Headstand. In case you are wondering why we always start with this posture, preceded only by the Rocking, the reason is that it is easier to balance while standing on your head when your body is not yet tired from other exercises. This time let us try the Headstand in the middle of the room, without the support of walls. Choose a place big enough for you to turn a somersault freely, for most likely this is exactly what you will do at first—more than once.

TECHNIQUE: First place a big pillow on the floor right in front of your exercise pad, kneel down before it, and do the Half-Headstand the way you have been doing it right along. Now make an additional step or two towards your head. Take a deep breath and, with a gentle bounce, get both legs off the floor and start slowly raising them, while still keeping the knees bent (see illustration).

The Headstand: (*Top Left*) First, assume the Half-Headstand position. (*Top Right*) Be sure to use arms, elbows, and hands for support. (*Bottom Left*) Start raising the legs slowly, knees still bent. (*Bottom Center*) Tuck in the buttocks for better balance. (*Bottom Right*) Slowly straighten the legs. (Photos by Jim Buhr)

Fifth Week

Just before straightening the legs, tuck in the buttocks, otherwise they will keep weighing you over and you will not be able to stay up. Also remember to keep the elbows not too far apart, as the whole body is supported by the head and forearms, not by the head alone. Now straighten your legs. If next you find yourself on the other side of the pillow after an unexpected somersault, don't be alarmed: get up and try again and again until you are able to maintain your balance. This may take several days, but do not get impatient and under no circumstances try to get up on the head more than four or five times in succession, as it is too exhausting. After four or five attempts, successful or not, lie down and relax. Do not overdo it.

Once on your head, *keep spine and legs straight,* toes pointed and body *relaxed.* Close your eyes and do deep breathing. Remain in this upside-down position for a few seconds, then slowly start coming down, first bending the knees and lowering the legs until your feet reach the floor. Remember to keep the toes *inverted!* Stand up slowly, stretch both arms above your head, take a deep breath and lie down for a rest.

Don't ever remain standing on the head if you are not feeling comfortable. Come down at once, and start all over again.

I cannot emphasize often enough that the head, neck, shoulders and spine should not be strained. If you find yourself unable to lose the fear of getting into an upside-down position, it is wise to continue with the Half-Headstand until you feel you are inwardly ready to try the complete posture. Don't start with the attitude of bravely taking a jump into deep water, because you will only become tense and your attempt will fail. Try it only when feeling relaxed and self-confident, without any sense of fear, rush or strain; otherwise stand on your head in the corner or near the wall. Enjoy it. Never force the issue.

Since the various benefits and warnings concerning the Headstand have been given in previous lessons, please look them up to be sure that you make no mistakes.

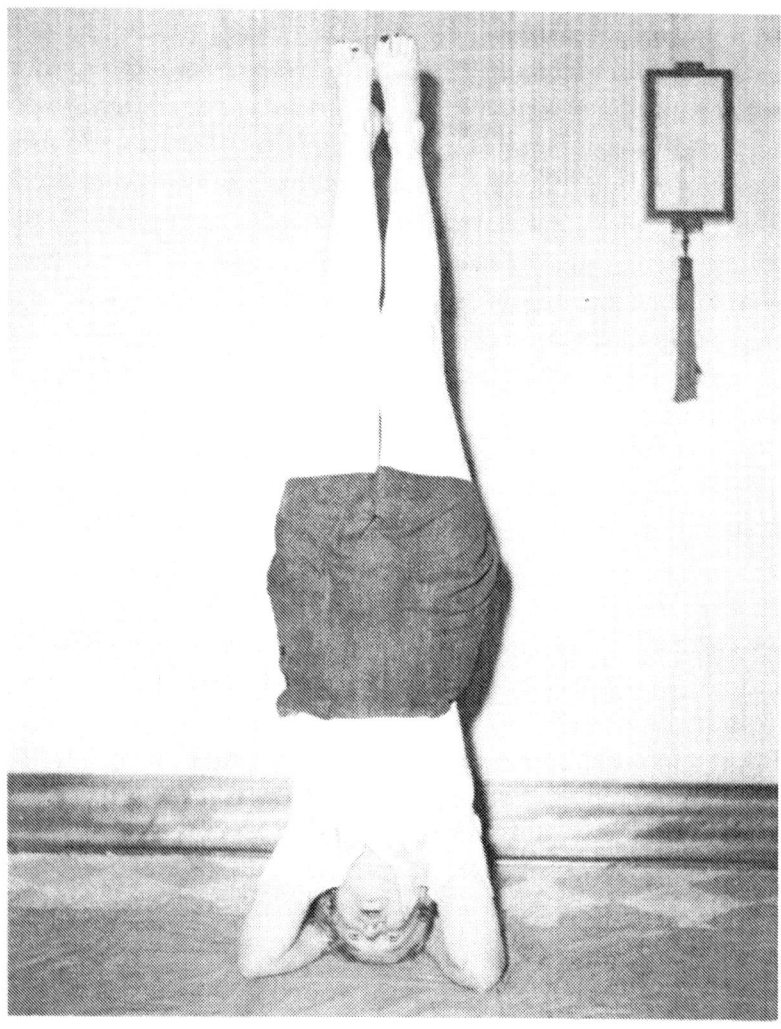

The Headstand, posed by the author's mother. (Photo by Jim Buhr)

TIME: Hold the Headstand for fifteen seconds at first, adding fifteen more per week. If the Headstand is done alone without any other exercise to precede or follow, it can eventually be

Fifth Week

done for fifteen to twenty minutes by an advanced student, otherwise the limit is twelve minutes.

The Triangle Pose

After taking a little rest, get ready to do the Triangle Pose, or *Oopavishta-Konasāna* in Sanskrit.

TECHNIQUE: Sit up straight and spread your legs sideways as wide apart as possible.

Inhale deeply, and while exhaling stretch out your arms and bend forward to the right till you can get hold of the toes of the right foot with both hands. Touch the right knee with your forehead. Retain this position, holding the breath; return to the sitting position and inhale.

Repeat the same movement, bending to the left, then to the middle. Now stretch out both arms sideways when starting the exhalation, at the same time bending your body forward until the hands reach the toes, the forehead touching the floor. If you cannot bend that far, simply bring your head down as low as you can. Use straps around the feet, or grasp your ankles if your hands cannot reach the toes.

TIME: To start with, keep this posture as long as you can hold your breath. Later on increase its duration to one minute,

The Triangle Pose, or *Oopavishta-Konāsana*, stretches both muscles and tendons. (Photo by Jim Buhr)

during which time you do deep breathing. Repeat two or three times.

The Twist Posture: Second Movement

We shall do now the second stage of the Twist Posture. I hope it will not present any difficulties after you have been practicing an easy version of it for a whole week.

Second movement of the Twist Posture, combined with deep breathing. (Photo by Mischa Pelz)

Fifth Week

TECHNIQUE: Start by assuming the familiar first stage of this Asana: First stretch out both legs, placing the right foot over the left knee. Now bend the left knee so that the left heel touches the right buttocks. Keep the left hand on the right foot as you did before, and wind the right arm around the back of the waistline, with your palm open. Take a deep breath and slowly make a complete turn to the right, keeping the shoulders straight and the chin up.

TIME: Retain the posture for ten seconds, then slowly straighten your head, shoulders, and chest. Do the whole exercise once more, then reverse the position of legs and arms and repeat the twisting movement to the left.

After that lie down to relax. When your breathing has returned to normal, take a few deep breaths.

The Shoulderstand

Now you will do the Shoulderstand, called *Sarvangāsana* in Sanskrit. Next to the Headstand, this posture is considered one of the best Asanas.

You see it done in many gymnasiums, beauty salons, and health clubs, but there it is seldom coupled with the deep breathing without which it is no longer a Yoga posture, but an ordinary exercise with much less therapeutic value.

It has been nicknamed "The Candle" because the body is kept as straight as a candle in this posture.

It is a very important Asana both for men and women, and should you imagine that you are "too old" to try it, just look at Ruth St. Denis—America's ageless dancer who posed for the picture. Though over eighty, she is doing the Shoulderstand with great ease and skill and practices it every day.

You will find it very similar to the Reverse Posture, with the difference that the body is kept in one straight line from shoulders to toes and the position of the hands is changed from the hips to the spine for better support. Moreover, the Reverse

Ruth St. Denis, over eighty years old, considers the Shoulderstand indispensable to her daily exercise routine.

Posture affects primarily the gonads, or sex glands, and partly the thyroid, whereas in the Shoulderstand the thyroid gland is influenced more and the gonads less.

TECHNIQUE: Lie down on your back and while inhaling deeply, slowly raise your legs until the toes point to the ceiling. Support the base of your spine with both hands and let the

Fifth Week

body rest on the nape of your neck and shoulders. Keep it as straight as a candle. Press the chin against the chest, straighten the knees and point the toes. Close your eyes and breathe deeply, trying to remain *steady* in this position.

Maintain the posture for several seconds, then while exhaling, *slowly* return to the lying position: First bend the knees, put the palms on the floor, then, curving the spine, gradually unfold it the way one unrolls a carpet. When your entire back touches the floor, straighten the knees, take a deep breath and slowly lower your legs to the ground *while breathing out*.

TIME: Retain the posture for from fifteen seconds to six minutes, adding fifteen seconds per week. If the Shoulderstand is done alone, without any other exercises to precede or follow, it can be retained from fifteen to twenty minutes by an advanced student.

BENEFITS: The Shoulderstand affects the thyroid gland and the sex glands and has, therefore, a powerful influence on the entire organism. It vitalizes the nerves, purifies the blood and promotes good circulation, strengthens the lower organs and helps them to stay in place. It is especially recommended for women after childbirth. People troubled by asthma, constipation or indigestion should diligently practice this posture. It is also helpful in overcoming painful menstruation, other female disorders, and seminal weakness.

CAUTION: The Shoulderstand should not be practiced by persons with organic disorders of the thyroid gland, and should be done cautiously by those troubled with chronic nasal catarrh.

The Supine Pose

A prolonged Shoulderstand sometimes produces a feeling of discomfort in the neck; you should therefore always follow it with the Supine Pose to relax the neck.

This pose somewhat resembles the Fish Posture, except for the position of the legs: instead of being crossed as in the Lotus

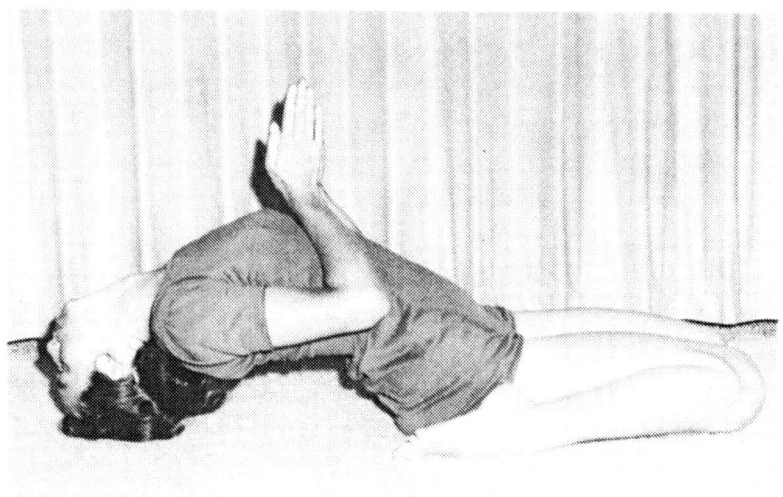

The Supine Posture relaxes the neck after the Shoulderstand. It tones both nerves and glands. (Photo by Jim Buhr)

Pose, they are kept on the sides as in the Supine Pelvic Posture. Since both of the above-mentioned postures have already been described in my previous book, you may prefer to learn a new one, which is a combination of the two.

TECHNIQUE: Kneel down, keeping knees together and feet apart with toes stretched. Now sit down on the floor *between* the heels, thus assuming the Pelvic Posture. Start reclining the body, leaning first on one, then on the other arm and elbow; throw the head far back. Continue the reclining movement until the top of your head rests on the floor. Keep the hands in the middle of the chest, palm to palm and finger tips up as at prayer.

Stay in this position for a while, breathing deeply, then return to the Pelvic Posture, leaning first on the elbows and arms, then on the palms. Relax for a while before starting with the breathing exercises.

TIME: Keep the posture from two to thirty seconds. Relax.

Fifth Week

BENEFITS: This posture affects the pituitary, pineal, thyroid and adrenal glands. It limbers and stretches the neck, strengthens and tones the nervous system, the kidneys, the stomach and intestines, the pelvic organs, and the nerves connected with sex functions.

BREATHING EXERCISES

The Recharging Breath

Now stand up, keeping the feet close together and holding the hands near the chest, with palms joined. Close your eyes and take several rhythmic breaths, visualizing how with every inhalation you draw in the vital cosmic energy, or Prana, and with every exhalation you send it circulating all over the body. A receptive mental attitude greatly helps the absorption of Prana from the air. Nor will the Prana "leak out," since you have closed the circuit, so to speak, by keeping your palms and feet together. Another variation of this exercise is done sitting in the Lotus Pose with palms placed on the upturned soles.

This exercise helps restore vitality when you feel as if all strength and life have left you. You can also use the Recharging breath for protecting yourself against the disturbing influences of gross or depressing vibrations. For this purpose it will suffice to keep together the thumb and third finger as if you were holding an invisible flower in each hand, then do the rhythmic breathing and at the same time visualize that you are building a protective circle around you.

In India one often does that when traveling a long distance by train with people whose vibrations might be of a low or an evil order. A friend of mine, a well-known artist in California, found himself doing it, too, when using subways and buses in New York, as he was so sensitive to alien vibrations that they would make him feel almost sick.

The Wood-Chopping Movement

Stand with your feet wide apart, stretch out your arms, clasp your hands, interlock the fingers and imagine yourself holding an axe. Inhale deeply, slowly raising your hands above your head until your body is swayed back. Remember that you are lifting a *heavy* axe. Hold the breath a moment, then, vigorously exhaling through the mouth, swing down with the axe in a powerful motion as if you were actually cutting wood. But instead of making an abrupt stop, let the arm swing a little after the first woodcutting movement.

Repeat this exercise several times, imagining that you are really chopping wood. Keep elbows and spine straight and don't move your buttocks when bending down. All the movement should be done by the spine from above the waist.

This exercise is very bracing and energizing and is also good for keeping the spine flexible and for reducing abdominal fat.

CAUTION: Persons with a weak heart and women suffering from female disorders should do this exercise very gently.

Finish the lesson with relaxation.

Fifth Week

The Woodchopping Movement: (a) Imagine yourself really lifting a heavy axe. (b) Let your arms swing in strong, rhythmic motion. (Photos by Jim Buhr)

ON THE YAMA-NIYAMA AND CONTEMPLATION

> *The way of the spirit is selflessness; the way of the body is selfishness. It is up to us to establish the balance between the two.*
>
> —SIGFRID KNAUER, M.D.

In India, before a Yoga aspirant is ready to begin his training he must accept, at least for the period of his discipleship, the *Yama* and *Niyama* which are the ten rules of the Yoga code of morals.

Yama consists of the following:

(1) inoffensiveness (non-destruction, non-injury);
(2) truthfulness;
(3) non-stealing;
(4) non-desire for what belongs to others;
(5) continence (frugality in diet, disinclination toward sexual enjoyment).

Niyama means:

(1) purification (internal and external cleanliness);
(2) contentment;
(3) strength of character (abstinence, forbearance, discipline, non-complaint, patience, calmness of mind);
(4) study;
(5) complete self-surrender to the Lord (which includes sharing with others that which has been given to you).

Certainly they must sound somewhat familiar to you. Do they not remind you of the Beatitudes and of the Ten Commandments?

But how many commandments and beatitudes do you still remember? Are you conscious of your own attitude toward them? Do you actually try to follow them? Or are you indifferent to them? Many people, for example, sincerely believe they

Fifth Week

are not guilty of killing. But were they to compare their reaction to the commandment, "Thou shalt not kill," with the attitude of, say, Albert Schweitzer, they would be forced to change their position. For Schweitzer does not allow *any* kind of killing in his jungle hospital in Equatorial Africa where he preaches "reverence for life"—not only for human life but for all life.

I was reminded of this, when I heard J. Allen Boone, who wrote *Kinship with All Life*,[1] telling us about the time when, just as he was about to spray his room in order to rid himself of ants, it suddenly occurred to him that they too were part of the Great Life and had a right to exist. After some hesitation he decided to talk to them, telling them that he respected their desire to live and would not kill them, yet since their proper place was outside in the garden, would they please leave. He gave them two days' "notice," warning them that he might be impelled to take measures if they refused to listen. "Believe it or not," he said in conclusion, "within two days the ants had actually disappeared."

This amusing story impressed me very much. Soon after this, Olga, our maid, discovered a stream of ants in the corner of the living room where a big night moth lay dead behind the curtains. Remembering Allen Boone's experience I asked her not to touch them, but to let me handle them. After she was gone I sat down on my knees to present my plight to the ants, asking them to go where they belonged and ending with a promise to keep some sugar for them outside. A few days later they were gone. "Because there is nothing to attract them," argued Olga; but when she lifted the curtain, we saw two more big moths lying on the floor and not a single ant around. Overwhelmed with joy I looked at her triumphantly.

This little incident opened up a vast new world for me. True,

---

[1] New York: Harper and Brothers, Publishers, 1954.

I know that some yogis, because they feel attuned to every living creature, can tame even tigers and other wild animals; but since I don't think of an ant as an animal, and I am not a yogini, I felt very elated when my gentle persuasion worked. From then on I started talking to all sorts of creeping and crawling things, which included a beautiful snake I encountered in the ruins of an ancient temple in Cambodia.

I am not so sure, of course, that I would be as successful with a tiger or a wild boar as I was with insects. So at this point we had better change the subject and return to Yama, which we were discussing.

I suggest you write down on a piece of paper the ten Yamas and Niyamas, or the Ten Commandments, or the Buddhist Commandments which are also ten in number. Here they are:

(1) Kill not, but have regard for life.

(2) Steal not, neither do ye rob; but help everybody to be master of the fruits of his labour.

(3) Abstain from impurity, and lead a life of chastity.

(4) Lie not, but be truthful. Speak the truth with discretion, fearlessly and in a loving heart.

(5) Invent not evil reports, neither do ye repeat them. Carp not, but look for the good sides of your fellow-beings, so that you may with sincerity defend them against their enemies.

(6) Swear not, but speak decently and with dignity.

(7) Waste not the time with gossip, but keep to the purpose or keep silence.

(8) Covet not, nor envy, but rejoice at the fortunes of other people.

(9) Cleanse your heart of malice and cherish no hatred, not even against your enemies, but embrace all living beings with kindness.

(10) Free your mind of ignorance and be anxious to learn the truth, especially in the one thing that is needed, lest you fall a prey either to scepticism or to errors.

I would suggest that every evening you take up just one point. Don't be in a hurry to answer it. Ponder about it and take time

Fifth Week

carefully to think over your answer before putting it aside.

A student of mine once cheerfully subscribed to the first Niyama, thinking that internal and external cleanliness were taken care of by tooth brushing and a daily bath. She had to reconsider, however, when it came to keeping the colon clean, and furthermore to cleansing the mind and heart of hatred, envy, jealousy, anger, malice, greed, and lust.

The last Yama concerns the sex life of the disciple, or *chela,* who is required to become a *brahmacharin,* or celibate, for the duration of his training. This, as you already know from our previous discussion on the Kundalini power, is necessary in order to conserve his sex energies so that they may be converted into finer energies, or *Ojas.* Except for this, the whole point of celibacy becomes useless. Yoga does not advocate the suppression of sex, but a sublimation of it. Remember, too, that all the strict rules and Yoga disciplines concern only a true disciple, not a student of Yoga such as you. But generally speaking the Yama-Niyama or the Commandments may well be taken into consideration by all human beings, especially so by those interested in spiritual advancement and understanding —not in their animal nature alone.

To recognize our own shortcomings and to see ourselves in a true light is a most difficult thing, more difficult than to do your hair, to shave, or make up and dress for a performance without a mirror. That is why we need an impartial third person such as a teacher to point out our faults to us. We cannot possibly see them ourselves, nor trust completely the criticism of our family or friends since, as is so often the case, they may all be prejudiced in one way or another.

What is one to do if there is no one to turn to for advice and guidance, no one to point out our wrongs to us, no one to tell us the truth about ourselves?

When, at one time, I found myself in such a situation— suddenly alone before I was ready to stand on my own feet, and surrounded by people to whom Yoga was nothing more than a target for jokes and uncomplimentary remarks—I remembered the advice once given me by Krishnamurti [2] in a desperate moment of my life, when I was going through very painful and distressing personal experiences.

"Do you know the real cause of your suffering?" Krishnamurti asked me then. "It is fear, although you may not realize it. You are unhappy because you are afraid to face your troubles and are trying to patch them up somehow. You want to run away from them instead of calmly examining what has caused your sorrow. You must face utter loneliness. If you really want to free yourself from the cause of your sorrow, you must be alone, and in facing that loneliness you will become watchful and alert. One is fully aware only when one is not trying to avoid something, nor trying to escape from the inevitable, which means to be alone. Through the ecstasy of that solitude you will realize the Truth."

He was right. When I began to analyze it, fear was at the bottom of my troubled state of mind. According to Krishnaji it was necessary to acquire a detached point of view; to see things from a different angle. But how was I to go about it? He advised me to remain completely alone and to see no one for several days. "Stay with your problem and look at it very closely. When you do that you will not be afraid of it any longer."

I followed his advice although I could not see how it was going to help me. Until then I had always thought that sympathy and warmth would help me more than solitude. I was wrong. After a few days spent alone in tears and despair a wonderful feeling of peace and joy suddenly entered my heart and filled my entire being. It seemed that all my torments be-

---

[2] Krishnamurti, reverently called Krishnaji in India, is widely known as a thinker, writer, and speaker. He is the author of *Education and the Significance of Life*, *The First and Last Freedom*, and *Commentaries on Living*.

Fifth Week

longed to a remote past; they meant no more to me now than the agonies of a crushed worm mean to a flying bird.

Later, recollecting the change this experience brought about in me, I resolved to keep regular days of complete silence, so that I might turn for advice and inspiration to that most reliable friend, teacher, and guide—the Over Self, the Truth within us. . . .

Setting aside a special time for this "meeting," I decided also to fast on the day of silence, to see no one and speak to no one, in short, to remain "absent" from everybody and everything.

In the beginning it felt a little strange to remain alone in my room in a sort of vacuum all day long. I had made it a point not to go on with my usual routine but spent the day meditating, listening to music and chants, reading the poems of Krishnamurti, books on Yoga and on the lives of great sages and saints. At times, I would just let thoughts pass by like the white clouds outside my window.

Soon after the beginning of the meditation I would become acutely aware of a presence that would fill the room like the blue smoke of incense. At first I would remain motionless, overwhelmed with joy at the visit of my unseen guest who soon became my judge, advisor and friend, one with whom I could frankly discuss all my troubles, difficulties, and shortcomings.

It is not difficult to solve a problem once you can see things from the detached point of view of an onlooker who is fully aware of the real, objective motives underlying every action. No cheating, no concealing, no twisting of facts is possible. One's most secret and hidden thoughts are brought to light and one's actions stand before one in all their nakedness. One knows then what is right and what is wrong, the reasons for having done this or the other thing, and what has brought about someone else's reactions.

Towards the end of the day I would generally break the

silence and the fast. Sometimes I kept it till the next morning, reluctant to leave the different world I had found. These days of silence, which I kept just once a month, became a great source of strength and inspiration to me during one of the most difficult periods of my life.

Once, when coming down from my room for a stroll in the garden, I happened to overhear our house boy answer the telephone: "Yes, Missi home" he was saying, "only she not talk, not eat today." A Chinese, he did not approve of this.

From time to time all of us should make a point of clearing our mental storeroom lest it become overcrowded with fears, unsolved problems, worrisome thoughts, suppressed emotions and thwarted hopes. We undoubtedly would be much better off if we did so. Usually we keep all this bottled up until finally something explodes either in the form of a nervous breakdown, a serious ailment, or a violent revolt of one kind or another.

Unfortunately, people are seldom capable of coming out with the whole truth—part of it invariably seems to get lost the moment one tries to put thoughts into words, whether because of fear or of shame at baring one's whole self to another person. But when you turn in all earnestness to the Higher Power within you, no pretense is any longer needed.

Should you find it impossible to arrange for a whole day of silence, try to spend a quiet half hour alone at the end of every evening, and let all your day's activities with their feelings, thoughts, and motives pass one by one before the Supreme Judge within you. Don't cover up anything. Do not justify your motives nor, above all, try to blame someone else for what has happened: make an honest effort to find out where *your* mistakes lie.

"I don't need to keep any special hour for silence," a woman once said to me, "since I live alone and have no one to talk to anyway." She had missed the whole point, of course, for one

Fifth Week

can actually remain alone for hours and days on end with the most trivial, superficial, and senseless thoughts, jumping from one to another like a grasshopper. If the hours of solitude are not utilized for introspection, contemplation and meditation, they have no special value and most likely will become a dreary, monotonous time.

A quiet evening's deep reflection, on the other hand, may enable you to look deep down into the "inner chamber" of self, see yourself as you really are, and thus come to recognize your faults and solve your problems. We know ourselves so little after all!

For instance, I know a woman whose cousin was so talkative that everybody in the family was ready to jump out of their skins. When gently told about the problem, she was hurt and simply refused to believe it, sincerely thinking of herself as a quiet person who seldom opened her mouth. Finally someone had the bright idea of setting up a tape-recorder, then playing it back to her. The effect was startling. The poor woman was completely crushed, realizing only then that she almost never closed her mouth.

Self-discipline is not as hard as one sometimes imagines and may even turn into an interesting experiment. We know of instant metamorphoses of sinners into saints, but in most cases we have to make a constant effort to remain alert. "Know thyself!" Difficult? Yes. But certainly something worth trying.

Now one last bit of advice: When reflecting upon your day's actions, thoughts, and words, dwell only on your misgivings, without counting your accomplishments. For accomplishments should come naturally and spontaneously. Otherwise you may end up by complimenting yourself for every trifle, like the little cub scout who, while putting down his good deeds for the day, wrote in all earnestness: "Got a chair for Grandmother!"

Lesson Six

SIXTH WEEK

Concentration is the source of strength in politics, in war, in trade, in short in all the management of human affairs.
—RALPH WALDO EMERSON

YOU ARE NOW STARTING ON THE FINAL WEEK OF YOUR YOGA course. You have learned a great deal in this short time and, let us hope, have derived some benefit from what you have learned. Your real task now will be to continue the daily practice of Yoga postures, not permitting yourself to grow lax simply because you have completed the lessons.

It is usually a good idea to do the exercises with a group at least once a week. This enables you to share your knowledge with others and also to continue perfecting yourself. Quite a few of my old students have formed such continuation groups. They meet weekly in someone's home, and if the attendance outgrows the size of the room they simply rent a small hall and share the expense. If you are at a loss as to how to contact interested people, try to do it through a newspaper or a health food store.

After finishing the course you will also have to decide on some sort of fixed schedule for your daily practice, and also choose which postures you are going to do every day and which you will leave for occasional practice.

Bear in mind that most important of all are the ten basic Asanas. You have learned them all in the past six weeks and you should keep them up. The other postures can be varied according to your requirements, time, and preference. Each person has his favorites. With some it is the Cobra, with others the Twist or Reverse Posture. The Headstand is a favorite with a great many people.

For you, the average Occidental with so many other things to do in the course of the day, the basic ten Asanas, two or three breathing exercises, and a few extra postures performed occasionally, will suffice to keep you in a healthy and youthful condition.

In India, the yogis usually favor about eighty-four Asanas, thirty-two of which are considered very beneficial, and ten are actually *essential* for the well-being of every individual. The original number of Yoga postures described in the old texts mounted to eighty-four thousand, but I doubt that any one among the living yogis today knows all of them.

Practice Schedule

Here is the order I suggest for your exercise schedule, unless you prefer some arrangement of your own that might be more suitable for your particular needs.

We shall not count the leg stretching exercise you are to do in bed before getting up. We shall begin with the *Rocking* exercise, the one you are supposed to do first of all, soon after arising. Next go on to the *Headstand,* which you should never skip under normal circumstances as it is the most valuable of all postures. I myself manage to do it even on a long plane journey, performing it while everybody is still asleep so as not to attract attention. My teacher, Sri Krishnamachrya, often used to say that one should stand on the head whenever tired, hungry, worried or sleepless. This, by the way, is not a para-

Sixth Week

dox. On the one hand, the Headstand can actually put you to sleep when you are suffering from insomnia; on the other hand, it acts as a refreshing tonic when you feel tired or low.

After the Headstand, do the *Shoulderstand* and either follow or precede it with the *Reverse Posture*. You can alternate these two, practicing the Shoulderstand one day and the Reverse Posture the next. Then comes the *Plough Posture,* which should be followed by the *Supine Pose*. The Supine Pose will relieve any tension in the neck that might have been produced by the Shoulderstand and the Plough, which is the reason for putting it in here. If you are familiar with the *Fish Posture* from my previous book, you can alternate it with the Supine Pose.

Next do the *Yoga Mudra*. If you are not yet able to assume the *Lotus Pose,* practice the Knee Bouncing first. Follow this with the *Stretching Posture.* After that get into the *Twist,* then the *Cobra,* and do the *Abdominal Lift* as the last.

Now you can do any of the other Asanas for which you have the time and inclination.

Do not forget to rest between the exercises. Give most time to those postures which you feel are most beneficial to you, even if these are not among the basic Asanas. Always finish up with a few of the breathing exercises and the Relaxation.

The Angular Rest Pose

Now let us try something new, the *Angular Rest Pose* or *Soopta-Konāsana.*

TECHNIQUE: First lie down and assume the Plough Posture, then move both legs as far apart as possible, keeping the knees straight. Get hold of your toes by inserting index and third fingers between the big and second toes.

TIME: Retain this position for about ten seconds and breathe deeply. Then bring the feet together again, put the arms down and start slowly to uncurve the spine in order to return to the lying position. Take a little rest.

The Angular Rest Pose combines the benefits of the Shoulderstand with those of the Plough Posture. (Photo by Jim Buhr)

BENEFITS: The Angular Rest Pose combines the benefits of the Shoulderstand and the Plough Posture. It is also a good exercise for acquiring a sense of balance.

The Angular Balance Pose

TECHNIQUE: Sit up straight with knees bent, keeping the feet sole to sole. Hook index and third fingers around the big toes as you did in the previous posture. Take a deep breath. On exhalation raise the feet off the floor and start very slowly stretching them sideways until both knees and elbows are completely straight. Do not slant the body: it should rest balanced on the lower part of the spine, or coccyx.

Remain motionless in this position for about ten seconds, breathing deeply. Then, still holding on to your toes, give the body a little jolt backwards. You will find yourself in the Angular-Rest Position once more.

TIME: Keep this pose for about ten seconds, careful to remain steady. Repeat several times, changing over from one position to the other and back without letting go of the toes.

In the beginning, you will find it difficult to hold yourself

Sixth Week

The Angular Balance Pose, a real triumph of balance for the advanced student. (Photo by Jim Buhr)

steady in either of the two postures, for as soon as you assume the sitting position you will be pulled back to the floor, while when trying to get into the Angular-Rest Position you will be pulled up again. In order to keep the body balanced in this pose, pick out a specific point on the floor, or anywhere in front of you, and gaze at it steadily.

The Twist Posture: Third Movement

The third and last movement of the Twist is done almost like the second, with only this difference: you change the position of the outstretched arm.

First, get into the second pose of the Twist, as given in Lesson Five: bend the left leg, place the right foot over the left knee, left hand on the right toes, right arm on the back of the waistline.

Now raise your left arm, place the elbow cap *on* the right knee and glide it down along the right side of the right thigh until you can reach the toes of the right foot with your left hand.

Then assume the Twist Pose by first inhaling deeply, then exhaling and twisting your head, shoulders and back to the right as you did before.

Repeat two or three times, then reverse the position of legs and arms and repeat the Twist to the left side.

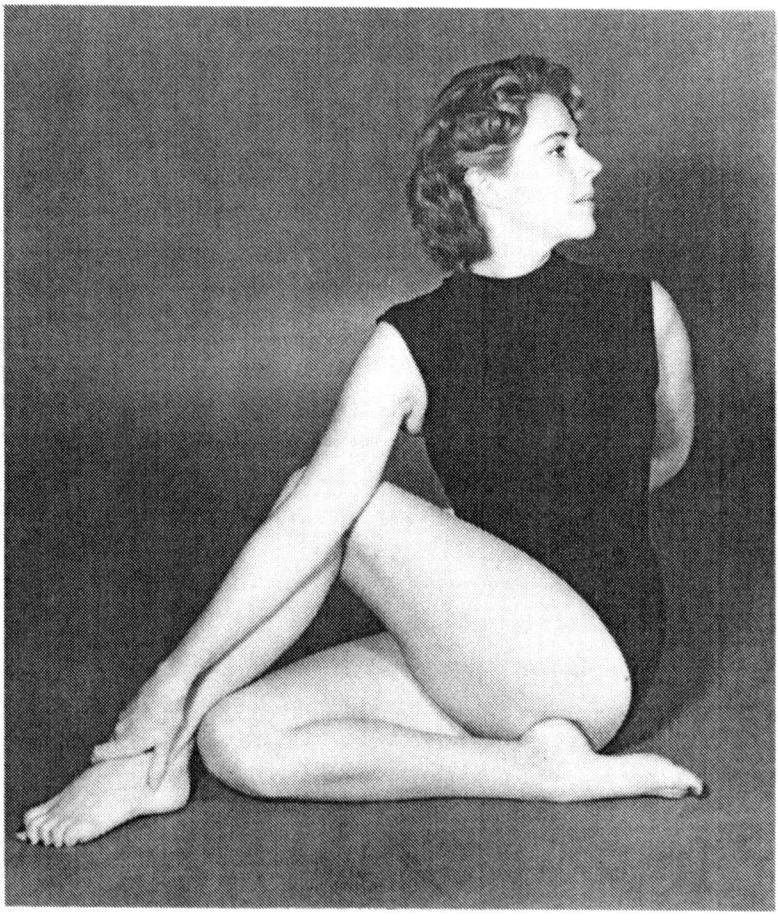

The Twist Pose: The third and final movement, demonstrated by actress Mala Powers. (Photo by Miller)

If you are unable to reach your toes, simply keep them up off the floor until you can master the correct posture, or put a strap around your toes and hold on to that.

The Twist gives a good many persons trouble at first. I remember the slim six footer, hero of many adventure films who wondered aloud in my class what was wrong with him. "Are my arms too short or am I too fat?" Neither was the case, of course. His limbs were just too stiff and his spine not flexible enough to accomplish this posture. "But I'll get into this position yet, even if I break my arms or my back trying," he announced, watching his wife and children do it with the greatest ease. He eventually did it, too, without the slightest injury. But it took time.

BREATHING EXERCISES

The Mountain Pose

Assume the Lotus Pose or sit with both legs crossed tailor-fashion. Raise the arms, interlock the fingers, then twist your hands so that your palms face the ceiling. Straighten the elbows. Do deep breathing while remaining in this position.

Another variation is done as follows: Kneel down, keeping your body straight from the knees up; stretch the arms up above your head, keeping the elbows straight and the palms joined, and do the breathing in this position.

The third variation is quite difficult and you need not feel too badly if you are not able to hold this position: First assume the Lotus Pose, then raise the buttocks off the floor and balance the body on the knee caps. Both hands should be stretched out above your head without the fingerlock, or else with palms joined.

This posture, in all its variations, is called "The Mountain Pose," *Parvatāsana* in Sanskrit.

The Mountain Pose, or *Parvatāsana*. First Variation (*Top Left*): Begin with the Lotus Pose, or else seated tailor-fashion. Second Variation (*Top Right*): Simplest of the three, it is done in the kneeling position. Third Variation (*Bottom Left*): Derived from the Lotus Pose, this takes considerable practice. (Photos by Jim Buhr)

Sixth Week

It is important to keep the outstretched arms steady while doing rhythmic breathing.

Second Breathing Exercise

Face the wall. Stretch out your arms, leaving a space of a few inches between your fingertips and the wall. Then, keeping your whole body as stiff as a board, place both palms on the wall, arms outstretched and elbows straight—this will tip your body slightly forward. Take a deep breath. While exhaling, slowly bend your elbows until your forehead reaches the wall. Keep your heels flat on the floor as you do this. Now inhale again while straightening your elbows and pushing your body away from the wall; exhale again while bending elbows. Repeat this to and fro movement several times.

Always remember to keep your body completely stiff. The normal tendency is to bend a little in the waistline, which ruins the effect of the exercise. Your only movement should be that of alternately bending and straightening elbows.

After a few days you may try to do this exercise faster. Do it as follows:

Take a deep breath, and do several of these push-ups against the wall while holding it, then exhale. Rest, then repeat. This

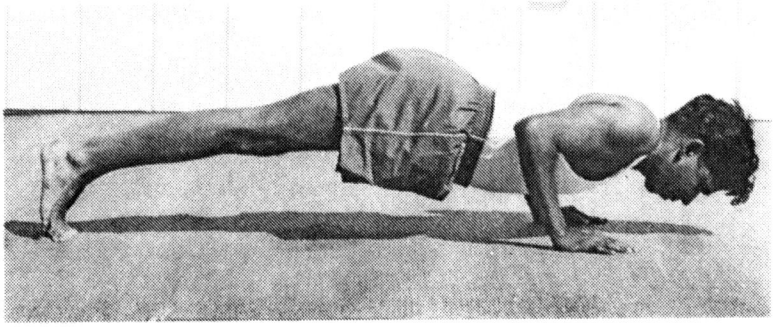

The Second Breathing Exercise resembles simple pushups in technique. (Photo by Jim Buhr)

exercise reduces fatty forearms and ankles and strengthens them. It also develops the chest and firms the muscles of the bust, forearms, and calves.

Still more effective, but more difficult and strenuous, are the same push-ups done on the floor instead of against the wall.

After practicing this exercise against the wall for some time, you should be able to do it on the floor without immediately falling flat on your abdomen.

Lie down on your stomach, keeping the toes inverted and palms on the floor at shoulder level. Take a deep breath and, while holding it, straighten and bend the elbows alternately, keeping your body stiff and motionless. Then, while exhaling, lower yourself slowly to the ground, chin and chest first, abdomen last. Do not neglect to concentrate on correct breathing.

Finish the lesson with the Relaxation.

ON CONCENTRATION AND MEDITATION

> *When the mind has become poised, the Self appears in its true state and we do not have to make any effort to perceive it.*
>
> —SWAMI PARAMANANDA,
> *Concentration and Meditation* [1]

The topic for the concluding talk in our course will be concentration and meditation, for these form an essential part of the training of a Yoga student.

What is the basic difference between concentration and meditation? In concentration, one involves only the mind; in meditation one involves the heart and the whole being as well.

"Concentration," to quote Patanjali's *Yoga Aphorisms* "is holding the mind steadily fixed on some particular object. Meditation is a continuous flow of thought on that object." In concentration you stay "on this side" of the particular object, in meditation you go beyond the limits of earthly manifestations. Whether you are a Christian, a Buddhist, a Hindu, whether you belong to some other religion or to none at all, the source of meditation is always of a spiritual nature.

The ability to concentrate is the mark of genius; the ability to meditate is the mark of saintliness.

Degrees of depth of concentration and meditation naturally vary with the individual. One person is able to keep his mind undistracted for only several seconds at a time, whereas another can do it for hours on end; this depends upon the natural gifts and training of each. Unfortunately, the art of concentration is seldom cultivated or taught in the West. This is especially true in America, where everything possible is done to provide constant distractions for the mind, which eventually dissipates

---

[1] Cohasset, Mass.: The Vedanta Centre.

itself. Overburdened with too many superficial and nonessential ideas, our mind finally loses the ability to concentrate, discern, and discriminate.

As a result, more and more people here never form the habit of thinking their own thoughts, making their own decisions, solving their own problems. They grow into emotionally immature men and women, who are unable to draw upon their own inner resources, and become completely dependent upon what other people do, say or think. Like small children, they begin to look for external diversions or what they consider thrills to break the monotony of their empty and meaningless existence. Here I suggest you look into *How to Live 365 Days a Year* by Dr. John A. Schindler,[2] a book from which I have quoted earlier. It will help you gain a better understanding of the people around you and of their behavior.

Our mind is actually almost the sole source of our pleasures and pain, failures and success, well-being and ills. This is true to a large extent of physical ailments as well. About eighty per cent of our diseases are said to be psychosomatic in origin. This fact alone speaks louder than any words, since it means that out of every ten sick people eight suffer from illnesses *originated* in the mind, whether by fear, worry, anger, jealousy or other hostile emotions.

This does not imply that the resultant suffering and pain are not completely real even when emotionally induced. Symptoms may often be treated medically. Yet any radical cure can only be effected through the mind, since that is the seat of the basic causes of illness.

For some reason most people, especially men, resent being told that their condition is due to emotional stress. "Ridiculous," snapped one businessman who came to see me. "If I can't sleep, it's just on account of these damned shingles, and

---

[2] Englewood Cliffs, N.J.: Prentice-Hall, Inc., 1954.

Sixth Week

my doctor told me that Yoga-breathing and relaxation might help. I am not a hysterical woman—I'm a sound businessman, a successful one at that!" However, a talk with him revealed that he was not nearly so invulnerable as he thought he was. He admitted he had been overworking of late, that business wasn't as good as it used to be, that he felt tired at times, and that a misunderstanding he had with a brother, who was also his business partner, had hurt him deeply. When we finally discovered that his shingles had first appeared on the day following their argument, I managed to persuade him to have a frank talk with his brother although at first he would not hear of it. As was to be expected, his troubles vanished as soon as his mind was put at ease, and he not only was able to sleep soundly again but got rid of the shingles as well.

The mind often behaves like a mischievous monkey that will play all sorts of tricks on us unless we watch it carefully. To illustrate, let us go and watch a Mr. John Brown as he gets ready to go down to breakfast after a rather disturbed night. We come upon him as he searches for the belt to his jacket. He is getting more and more annoyed. Finally, giving up his search, he goes down for coffee in the garden. To his surprise, he sees his belt lying in the grass under his bedroom window. Pleased to have found it at last, he starts to pick it up when his wife cries, "It's a snake, be careful!" Stepping back quickly, he collides with the maid who drops the breakfast tray. The hot coffee spills not only over the new jacket but also on Mr. Brown's little son who has come tricycling over to see the snake, and who now starts crying bitterly. At last the gardener, alerted by all the commotion, arrives with a big shovel to kill the snake. He stops and grins broadly. "That's no snake—that's the old garden hose I threw away this morning." And that is what it actually was all the time. So you see, our Mr. Brown's joy ("Ah, there is my belt!"), and his fear ("It's a snake!") were only imaginary. But the consequences of his mind-tricks were very real: his little boy is covered with blisters, the china is broken to pieces and the new jacket is soiled, not to mention a badly spoiled morning for everybody.

Who is to be held responsible for all this? Mr. Brown? His son? The gardener? The maid? She is probably the one who will be blamed in the end for "running into" Mr. Brown with the tray, while the real culprit—his mind—will escape unsuspected.

Yet if Mr. Brown's mind had been calm and objective in the first place, he would not have been so easily irritated, excited, and frightened in turn, nor would his imagination have so quickly turned the old hose first into a belt, then into a snake.

If we knew how to concentrate and use our minds, our life would often be very different. We would not only be free of our daily fears, but would also make a success of almost everything we chose to do, whether in the field of art, science, business, politics, or personal relations.

A person who has mastered the art of concentration usually also develops a magnetic, vibrant, and inspiring personality to which people are easily drawn.

Take the biography of any successful man, and you will find that even if he started his career without money or education, yet he always possessed one important quality, namely the ability to concentrate. Without this quality he could never have been a success.

Concentration can be taught to a child through games as soon as he begins to think independently, at the age of about six or seven. I recall one such game we used to play in my family. It was a guessing game. One of us would pretend we had been given a certain sum of money with which to buy whatever we pleased, except that it must be neither black or white in color. We were also not allowed to answer "yes" or "no" to the questions the others asked while trying to guess what we had bought. It took a lot of concentration for a child

Sixth Week 173

not to say "yes" when asked whether she liked the dress she had bought, or refrain from saying "no" when questioned whether it wasn't a white one.

There are dozens of such games which may be played with children, provided the grown-ups are not too busy, too lazy, or too disinterested.

Interesting experiments with thought-projection have been conducted here in Los Angeles by a prayer group formed by Franklin Loehr, who showed us some astounding results produced by the influence of concentration on plant life. He had, for instance, a large container covered by lush greenery on one side, while the other half was completely barren—just plain earth. We were told that an equal amount of seeds had been planted on both sides of the container and that both sides had been given exactly the same attention, with only one exception: the group had been praying regularly for the seeds on the right side to grow and live and for those on the left side to wither and die. This experiment, in case you wish to refer to it, is recorded in *The Power of Prayer on Plants*.[3]

The question of whether it is right to pray for the destruction of any life, even plant life, is another matter, and one we are not discussing here. Nor will we discuss the fact that during a war both sides pray regularly for the victory of their own armies and the destruction of the enemy!

The power of positive thinking undoubtedly works. But so does the power of negative thinking. Like electricity, the power itself is neither positive nor negative; it simply exists, and it is up to us human beings to put it to use one way or another. That is why in Yoga concentration is usually preceded by Yama-Niyama and followed by meditation. Both, it is felt, safeguard the student from possible misuse of his thought-power.

---

[3] The Reverend Franklin Loehr, *The Power of Prayer on Plants*, New York: Doubleday & Company, Inc., 1959.

With most people the driving force behind concentration is usually desire. When a person desires something passionately, he automatically concentrates upon it and drives towards the achievement of his goal. The goal itself may be creative or destructive, but in either case desire is the force urging its realization, and a person will use concentration to overcome the various obstacles in his path. Concentration is a powerful double-edged weapon which can cut for you or against you, depending on how you use it. Therefore we must always be aware of the real motives directing our actions and creating our problems.

"Awareness is the silent and choiceless observation of *what is*," says Krishnamurti. "In this awareness the problem unrolls itself and thus it is fully and completely understood." [4]

The often-suggested method of self-improvement through the substitution of one emotion for another is likely to breed hypocrisy, whereas if we become acutely and honestly aware of our shortcomings, a change of heart often takes place and transforms us almost instantly. This was true of the Apostle Paul, of Mary Magdalen and countless others of whom we may never have heard. This, too, is how some alcoholics give up liquor and heavy chain smokers their cigarettes.

An elderly woman who used to be crippled with arthritis recently told me that someone had once said to her that she would never get better so long as she continued to hate the people around her. She was intelligent enough to listen, and once she became fully aware of her faults she changed almost overnight. Before long she was able to leave her wheel chair and go back to work.

The great majority of people live in total unawareness of the real cause of their miseries, drudgery, and unhappiness. When still in Russia and a girl in my teens, I learned an un-

---

[4] Jiddu Krishnamurti, *Commentaries on Living,* New York: Harper and Brothers, Publishers, 1956.

Sixth Week 175

forgettable lesson from a friend who used to write to me from a dull provincial town where his regiment was stationed. In one of his letters he said that since he had no interesting people to talk to and no good books to read, he had made friends with the sun, moon, and stars, with the birds, trees, and flowers. "Every day I talk to them and listen to their fascinating stories. And then, when we fall into silence, it seems to me that I can perceive the gentle image of Christ smiling through them to me. Thus I live in constant awareness and expectation, treating every day as though it were the last of my earthly existence. Everything then appears in a different light and acquires a greater meaning. I am never bored, lonely or unhappy: I have learned to live in the eternal Now."

Awareness born of solitude and meditation gives one a new and different understanding of life. You too may, during a quiet evening of reflection, find that you are suddenly able to look deep down into the "inner chamber" and see yourself in a true light, "as you are." All of us can profit by such an experience since all of us know ourselves so imperfectly. A despot, for instance, seldom thinks he is tyrannical, a miser does not believe he is stingy, a chatterbox is not aware of talking incessantly.

During one of my recent lectures someone in the audience asked me to define the difference between prayer and meditation. In prayer, one usually asks a favor, thereby creating a division between the asker and the one who is being asked, the begger and the giver. In meditation, one does not ask for anything. Swami Sivananda, in *Practical Guide for Students of Yoga*,[5] calls meditation "the flow of continuous thought of one thing or God." It is directed to the higher being within. In order to be able to meditate we must first develop the ability to concentrate, to keep our minds still and steady.

---

[5] Hong Kong: Divine Life Sty.

The first step in concentration is the practice of Yoga postures, deep breathing and relaxation.

"One who has not proper control over his body cannot make proper use of his mind, he can never concentrate—much less can he meditate. A man who lacks mastery over his physical organism cannot possibly gain spiritual consciousness; hence the need to practice posture," writes Swami Paramananda in *Concentration and Meditation*.[6]

Since our mind is in a perpetual state of restlessness and motion, we cannot succeed in keeping it quiet without a certain amount of training. If you, or any other person who has had no previous experience, were asked to concentrate for just five minutes on a single object, you would probably find yourself unable to do so: your thoughts would start drifting after the first few seconds.

Supposing you were to concentrate on a red rose. First you would look at it with your mind's eye, admiring its beauty, warm color and soft, velvety leaves. Then another thought would probably cut in: "How like my new velvet dress . . ." or something to that effect. Your thoughts would leave the rose and drift in another direction: "That dress looked very effective the other night at Peter's farewell party. . . . Silly boy, he asked me to think of him while he is in Germany. . . . Why do they send our boys to Germany anyway? . . . the Frauleins there are bound to get hold of him. . . . Peter said that Japanese girls make the best wives. . . . They looked quite cute in the film on Japan. . . . Do all women there carry babies on their back? . . . Mary once sent me a picture postcard from Australia that showed a kangaroo with a baby in its pouch . . . She said Sydney was a big place . . ." and so on and so forth until the red rose on which you started to concentrate is completely forgotten.

---

[6] Cohasset, Mass.: Vedanta Centre.

Sixth Week

The same thing, with infinite variations of course, is likely to happen to almost every beginner. During the few minutes of his concentration period he will have to discipline his thoughts again and again, like so many monkeys on a leash. As soon as you notice your thoughts beginning to stray, rein them in and return to the object of your concentration.

Every normal human being possesses the faculty of concentration, but we seldom know how to apply it consciously. Most of us use it automatically and instinctively. Only after we have gained command over our mental and spiritual forces do we learn to concentrate successfully.

It has been my experience that for a beginner the most suitable object for concentration is the light of a burning candle. Before you begin, select a quiet place where you are not likely to be disturbed. Then choose a comfortable position in which you can sit at ease, keeping the spine erect. You may assume any of the meditative poses I have outlined or merely sit cross-legged. Use a chair if you prefer, but remember to straighten your back.

Then light a candle and, your gaze fixed steadily upon the light, start on your rhythmic breathing. Look at nothing except the flame—neither at the candle itself, nor at the wall behind, nor at any other object. Do not stare, however, and do not tense up—remain inwardly relaxed though motionless.

Let a minute pass, then close your eyelids but continue to envision the flame with your inner eye. In other words, you must be able to *see* the flame uninterruptedly, even with your eyes closed. If you cannot successfully capture the vision of the flame, or if it vanishes too quickly, immediately reopen your eyes, look at it, then close them again. Repeat this several times until you are able to capture *and hold* the vision of the flame. Resume the rhythmic breathing from time to time.

Now begin reflecting upon the qualities of the flame, upon its color, its shape. Look at it with a warm feeling of affection.

Ponder on its symbolical meaning as representing the eternal divine Light. Thus you begin to meditate on the light.

After a few days it will no longer be necessary to light the candle. You will be able to visualize the flame by simply closing your eyes and concentrating on it. To start with, set aside some five to ten minutes a day for the practice of concentration.

The next stage of meditation is more difficult: You start by concentrating on the light as you have been doing so far. Then dismiss it and do the rhythmic breathing for about half a minute. Imagine now that the light which you have been contemplating is no longer outside but within you. Place it right in the sacred chamber of your heart and let it shine there, brightening every dark corner, sending out warmth and friendliness in all directions, to every living being. Let the flame in your heart grow bigger and brighter all the time, dispelling the darkness of loneliness, fear, hatred, anger, envy, jealousy, greed and lust . . . dispersing disease and pain . . . giving you health, strength and courage, becoming the source of love, compassion, and happiness.

When finally the light in your heart permeates your entire being and you have become one with it, you will attain a union with the eternal divine Light which is Love, which is Truth, which is God.

In a week or so, after you have succeeded in visualizing the candle flame without difficulty, you may change to something else or take up another object in addition to it.

It is not advisable, however, to make this change before you are able to concentrate successfully or meditate on the first object you had chosen. Abandon it only when you find that it is too hard for you to hold your attention on it.

One of my students, for instance, had great difficulty in concentrating on an apple because after visualizing it he instinctively felt like eating it. In a case like this, one should not try to persist. Dismiss the object and replace it by another one.

Sixth Week

Always choose something beautiful and pleasant to concentrate on.

When you notice that you have begun to make good progress, you can start concentrating and meditating on abstract matters, on various qualities and ideas. But be doubly careful to select only those which are positive, right, noble and elevating.

"We must not remain content with lower forms of concentration," writes Swami Paramananda.[7] "These may bring us physical health, prosperity or success, because concentration always gives power; but even though we acquire more wealth, greater honor or increase bodily strength, we shall find that one part of our being still remains unsatisfied in spite of all our worldly acquisitions. Never will it be content until we awaken and begin to work for our higher development."

As concentration gives added power, we should be very careful in choosing what we want, so that we do not concentrate on the fulfillment of base or selfish desires.

It is not always easy to determine whether our wish is selfish or not. Is the wish to be healthy, for instance, a selfish one? Is the desire to marry a person you love selfish?

Therefore, whenever making a wish, we should add "if it is right for me." By doing so, we do not superimpose our will upon the Higher Will. In other words, we say, "Thy will be done." But if we are bent on getting what *we* want, we may find eventually that it was the worse thing that could have happened to us; we simply didn't know it at the time we were in pursuit of it.

It is only through proper and unselfish meditation that the student can finally enter the temple of the undistracted mind, and in silence and aloneness come to the realization of the One Ultimate Reality and the peace beyond understanding.

---

[7] *Op. cit.*

Appendix I

DISCUSSION OF DIET AND RECIPES

MANY OF MY STUDENTS AND READERS HAVE ASKED ME TO OUTLINE a diet for them. As I have already pointed out in Lesson Two, this is difficult to do since food requirements and tastes vary not only with the individual but also with one's age. Here, for instance, is my own diet, which would hardly satisfy most people, partly because I am a vegetarian and partly because I take only one meal a day—for breakfast and dinner I eat very little.

UPON ARISING:	A glass of water which has been kept overnight in a copper tumbler, taken with or without lemon.
BREAKFAST:	A cup of soya-bean milk or cereal coffee. Some almonds and raisins. A grapefruit or orange eaten with the white rind and part of the skin (the fruit organically grown and free of poisonous spray), or a papaya.
BETWEEN MEALS:	I drink plenty of water, some fresh fruit and vegetable juices, and eat fruit in season.
LUNCH:	Soup Green salad with or without dressing

	1 cooked vegetable *or* 1 raw vegetable *or* a serving of any one of the following: cooked soya bean curds, brown rice, or groats, *or* a baked potato with oil or butter and soya sauce or vegetable salt (the skin of the potato is included).
EVENING MEAL:	A cup of cereal coffee with honey
	A sliced tomato with cheese or egg yolk *or* yogurt with honey and wheat germ *or* a slice of whole grain or whole wheat bread with avocado and vegetable salt.
BEFORE RETIRING:	A glass of water.

Since the Hay Diet, which gets its name from its originator, Dr. William Howard Hay, has been brought again to the attention of the public, I have had repeated requests to explain it. This diet classifies foods so that carbohydrates are separated from proteins and from acid and sulfur-content foods; they are not to be eaten together at any one meal. The reason for this is that alkaline-forming foods and acid-forming foods each require different conditions for their proper digestion.

Starch should be well masticated, so that it may be converted into glucose by the saliva before it leaves the mouth—in the stomach it lies almost idle until it passes through the duodenum into the intestine where it is digested again. Protein, on the contrary, is digested mainly in the stomach, where gastric juices begin to secrete as soon as the protein reaches it. If carbohydrates are present in the stomach at the same time, they start fermenting because the acid in the gastric juices affects the starch, thereby creating gas and acidity. The same thing happens when starch is eaten together with foods containing acid, such as lemons and other citrus fruits, tomatoes or vinegar, or with sulfurous food such as cabbage, peas, beans, cauliflower, Brussels sprouts or eggs. This classification of foods is especially beneficial for people suffering from indigestion and gas.

Discussion of Diet and Recipes

The Hay Diet Food Classification

Items from columns A & B do not combine with each other. Neutral items combine with both.

A		B
PROTEINS	NEUTRAL	STARCH
Brains	Artichokes (cone)	Artichokes (Jerusalem)
Buttermilk	Asparagus	Bread (whole grain)
Cheese	Beans (snap)	*Bread (white)*
Clams	Beans (dried) *	Cereals (whole grain)
Crabs	Beans (green) *	*Cereals (refined)*
Eggs	Beet tops	Chestnuts, cooked
Fish	Broccoli *	Corn (mature)
Game	Brussels sprouts *	Corn starch
Gelatin	Cabbage	Flour (whole grain)
Meats	Cauliflower *	*Flour (white)*
Milk	Celery	*Gravies (white flour)*
Nuts	Chard	*Macaroni*
Oysters	Corn (tender)	Oatmeal
	Dandelion greens	*Pastries*
FRUIT	Eggplant	Peanuts
	Kale	Popcorn
Apples	Kraut	Potatoes (in jackets)
Apricots	Leeks	*Sago*
Berries	Lentils *	Rice (whole)
Cherries	Lettuce	*Rice (polished)*
Currants	Lima beans	*Spaghetti*
Grapes	(green) *	*Soup, with white flour*
Grapefruit	Mushrooms	*thickening*
Kumquats	Okra	*Tapioca*
Lemons	Onions *	
Limes	Peas (green) *	SWEETS
Mangoes	Peas (dried)	
Oranges	Peppers (green)	*Candies*
Peaches	Pumpkin	*Ice-cream (commercial)*
Pears	Spinach	*Jellies*
Prunes	Squash	*Jams*
Pineapple	Vegetable marrow	*Preserves*
Plums		*Syrup refined*

Pomegranates
Tangerines
Tomatoes
Raisins

ROOTS

Beets
Carrots
Celery
Kohlrabi
Mangelwurzel
Parsnips
Radishes
Rutabagas
Turnips

SALADS
  and
LETTUCE (all
  kinds)

Chicory
Chives
Cucumber
Garlic
Onions (green)
Parsley
Watercress

White sugar

FATS (not more than three in one meal)

Avocado
Butter
Coconut
Cream
Egg yolks
Fats (animal)
Lard
Nuts
Oils

SUGARS (not more than two in one meal)

Bananas (ripe)
Dates
Figs
Honey
Maple sugar
Maple syrup
Prunes
Raisins
Sugar (raw, brown)
Persimmons

Italicized items are not recommended at all. Items marked with an asterisk may be eaten together with salads, vegetables or fruit as a main course, provided no other proteins or starches are included. They are not recommended for people suffering from gas. Cabbage should not be eaten by people troubled by indigestion.

As already mentioned, no *cooked* sulfur foods such as cabbage, cauliflower, turnips, peas, beans, etc., are to be combined with starches, as this produces gas.

Discussion of Diet and Recipes

Lean meat, game, poultry, liver, kidneys, heart, sweetbreads and fish may be eaten prepared in any way except fried or with the addition of breadcrumbs or sauces and gravies thickened with flour.

Cleansing Diet

There are several good ways to cleanse the system. One way is to stay from five to ten days on a mono diet, that is, to eat as much as one likes of any one of the following:

(a) Watermelon—especially good for cleansing the kidneys. If you feel too hungry, eat a slice of whole wheat bread or whole wheat wafers.
(b) Grated raw apples and herb tea with lemon—especially good for people suffering from dysentery, colitis or sprue. (The apples should be grated on plastic, glass or stainless-steel graters.)
(c) Fresh grapes, unsprayed, in order to avoid danger of poisoning. This mono diet is beneficial for the liver.
(d) Coconut water only—cleanses the liver and alkalizes the system.
(e) Papaya with lemon juice—very good for the intestinal tract.
(f) Grapefruit and/or orange juice—alkalizes the system.

A less rigid cleansing diet was sent me by one of my students who lives on a farm near New York City, where she grows her own vegetables and fruit. By doing the Yoga breathing exercises and Yoga postures and keeping this diet, she completely overcame a bad asthmatic condition. Here it is:

Health Diet

ON ARISING: 1 glass of water with fresh lemon juice.

BREAKFAST: Any herb tea *or* coffee substitute *or* raw cow's, goat's, butter-, or soya-bean milk.
Whole grain cereal sweetened with honey or date or raw sugar, *or* 1 slice whole grain bread

APPENDIX I

with date or almond butter *or* small dish of stewed fruit *or* any fresh fruit in season.

BETWEEN MEALS: Water

Fruit *or* vegetable juice *or* fruit eaten out of hand.

LUNCH: Buttermilk *or* herb tea *or* cereal coffee.

Salad made with any raw greens, including especially watercress and parsley, with a dressing made of juice of 1 lemon, vegetable salt and saf-flower, sunflower, sesame or soya-bean oil.

1 slice whole grain bread *or* baked potato.

Yogurt *or* cottage cheese *or* sour cream with any fruit.

DINNER: Herb tea *or* cereal coffee.

Vegetable broth.

Celery sticks, carrots and sliced cucumbers.

1 serving of either meat, fish, poultry, cheese, eggs or nuts.

1 serving of a vegetable grown above ground.

1 serving of a vegetable grown below ground.

Fresh fruit *or* stewed fruit *or* raisins and nuts.

Take a spoonful of saf-flower, sunflower, sesame, soya-bean or cod liver oil, four hours after your last meal.

Reducing Diet

UPON ARISING: One glass of water with fresh lemon juice.

LUNCH: Salad (no dressing except lemon juice).

1 cup of soup (no cream, butter or flour).

1 soft boiled egg or soya bean cake [1] *or* 3½ ozs. lean meat or fish, broiled, baked or roasted.

---

[1] Soya bean cake is known as *Tofu* in Chinese and Japanese restaurants and markets. As already mentioned, its protein content is higher than that of cheese, meat, milk, or eggs, and it is not acid-forming.

Discussion of Diet and Recipes

Celery sticks, raw carrots, radishes, cucumbers, etc.
Fruit in season.
Skim milk or buttermilk, 8 fl. ozs.

DINNER:
1 cup of soup.
1 boiled egg or piece of cheese.
½ cup serving of vegetable.
Salad (no dressing except lemon juice).
Skim milk or buttermilk, 8 fl. ozs., *or* yogurt.
½ cup serving of fruit.
Herb tea or cereal coffee with skim milk (no cream or sugar).

EVENING SNACK: Any kind of fresh fruit, fruit juice, or vegetable juice.

Diet for People Over Thirty-five

Our body reaches its full maturity around the age of twenty-eight. By the time we reach the age of thirty-five, the body gradually begins to decrease its activities and the life-processes slow down their pace.

Therefore, if we want to remain healthy and youthful we should accordingly make certain changes in our diet and eating habits so as not to overburden the digestive system with extra work.

After the age of approximately thirty-five we should start cutting down on all saturated fats such as lard, bacon, butter, nuts and nut butter, and on refined carbohydrates like bread, pastries, pies, macaroni and other products containing white flour and white sugar. We should eliminate them completely around the age of sixty, after which even eggs and potatoes should be eaten sparingly. The same is true of all other starchy and sulfurous foods which create gas when eaten together during the same meal. (See pages 183-184, the Hay Diet food classification.)

Fried food is never good for anyone, and should be given

up completely after the age of about thirty-five. Our food should be steamed or boiled,[2] baked or broiled. Raw foods like fruit and vegetables may be also juiced or grated, if desired.

A glass of water with lemon juice every morning and a pint of buttermilk a day should never be omitted. The following items are especially recommended for people over thirty-five: Buttermilk, cottage cheese, soya bean products (milk, *Tofu* or soya bean curds, cheese), fish, shrimps, oysters, lean meat; alfalfa sprouts, bell-peppers, carrots and carrot juice, fresh corn, dandelions, endive, parsley, romaine, watercress. Included also are foods that contain vitamins, minerals and protein in abundance, such as grapefruit, oranges, lemons, apricots, grapes, figs, dates, raisins, plums, prunes, boysenberries, strawberries, raspberries, cantaloupe, watermelon and papayas.

One of the best alkalizing drinks is potato water,[3] which helps the system to eliminate impurities. People suffering from arthritis are especially benefited by drinking potato water first thing in the morning, at least once during the day, and the last thing at night. They should also eat one or two finely-grated potatoes, skin included, every day. This may be added to salads, soups or vegetables directly before serving.

The Indians claim that people afflicted with arthritis should always keep a raw unpeeled winter-crop potato close to their skin. As soon as the potato becomes either very hard or very soft, it should be discarded and replaced by a fresh one. I myself have seen a woman who previously had hardly been able to move her fingers open and close her fists a week after she started playing around with a potato. She kept it in her apron pocket during the day, holding it in her hands whenever she had the chance. At night, to prevent the potato from rolling

---

[2] The best method is to cook over a slow fire, without water, in tightly covered stainless steel utensils.

[3] Wash 3 or 4 medium size, unpeeled potatoes and simmer, covered in 1 quart of water for about an hour. Strain through a cloth and drink the water.

Discussion of Diet and Recipes 189

away, she slipped her hand, with the potato in it, into a stocking.

Since there is no risk of any kind involved in holding a potato, and since you may even start a new fashion by wearing one around the neck like a medallion, you could safely try this experiment. Just be sure to remember that the potato must be a winter-crop one. And let me know the results.

Recipes

SALAD: One head romaine or any other green salad, except iceberg lettuce, which contains almost no chlorophyll
plus
Watercress, parsley, tomatoes, green onions, chopped celery, fresh cucumber, finely cut bell-peppers, alfalfa sprouts or bean sprouts, any herb, mint leaves, grated carrots or grated beets, in any combination desired.
Sunflower seeds or pinion nuts to taste (1-2 heaping tablespoons).

Combine the above ingredients, breaking the salad into small pieces by hand. Directly before serving add any of the following dressings:

Dressings:

(a) Lemon juice, oil, soya sauce or vegetable salt, honey, Sesame Tahini (available in health food stores), in any combination to taste. The general rule is about 2 parts oil to 1 part lemon juice.
(b) Sour cream with honey water.
(c) Oil, lemon, grated Roquefort cheese, in any combination desired.
(d) Egg yolk, lemon juice, salt, honey, in any combination desired.
(e) Buttermilk, grated onion, vegetable salt, a dash of curry powder.

SOUPS: *Cauliflower Soup:*

1 medium cauliflower
1 medium onion, chopped

1 medium carrot, diced
6 cups water
3 laurel leaves
Soya sauce to taste
Seasoning to taste

Boil carrot and bay leaves for about 15 minutes. Add cauliflower cut up into flowerets and the chopped onion. Simmer, covered, until cauliflower is tender. Remove laurel leaves. Season and serve. Serves 4 liberally.

Spinach Soup:

1 package chopped spinach
1 large carrot
1 medium onion, chopped fine
1 medium potato (optional)
4 cups water
3 laurel leaves
Juice of ½ lemon
Seasoning to taste
Hard-cooked eggs, 1 per serving

Simmer all ingredients, except lemon juice, together, tightly covered, for about half an hour. Add lemon juice and seasoning. Serve with sliced hard-cooked eggs. Serves 4 generously.

Carrot Soup:

4 medium carrots
1 large onion
4 cups water
2 laurel leaves
1 tablespoon oil or butter
Seasoning to taste
Chopped parsley for garnish

Combine all ingredients, bring to a boil and simmer, tightly covered, until vegetables are tender. Sprinkle with fresh parsley. Serves 4 generously.

Pea Soup:

¼ package split peas

Discussion of Diet and Recipes

1 whole large onion
1 medium onion, chopped and sautéed in a little oil
6 cups water
3 laurel leaves
Seasoning to taste

Combine all ingredients, except sautéed onion, bring to a boil and simmer, covered, for about an hour or until peas are soft. Remove laurel leaves and the whole onion. Add the cooked chopped onion and simmer a few minutes longer. Season to taste. Serves 4 generously.

ELECTRIC
BLENDER
RECIPES

Soups may also be made by using an electric blender. These soups will be ready within 10 or 15 minutes. Here are some recipes for such soups:

Carrot Soup:

4 medium carrots
1 large onion
1 laurel leaf
4 cups water
Seasoning to taste

Cut up onion and carrot and boil with laurel leaf for 5-6 minutes. Remove laurel leaf. Allow to cool off, put in blender and mix for 2-3 minutes. Put back on low flame for another 5 minutes. Season to taste. Add a little oil or butter if desired. Serves 4.

The above recipe may be varied according to your own preference. Here are a few suggestions:

Celery and Leek Soup:

¼ bunch celery, broken into small pieces, with strings removed
2 leeks, cut into pieces
1 medium potato
4 cups water
Seasoning to taste

Proceed as for Carrot Soup directly above. Serves 4.

Potato Soup:

2 medium potatoes, diced
1 onion, diced
4 cups water
1 laurel leaf (optional)
1-2 tablespoons oil or butter
Seasoning to taste

Proceed as for Carrot Soup made in blender. Serves 4.

Cauliflower Soup:

1 small cauliflower
1 onion
4 cups water
1 laurel leaf (optional)
Seasoning to taste

Proceed as for Carrot Soup made in blender. Serves 4.

VARIOUS
DISHES: *Cauliflower Casserole:*

1 large cauliflower
2 medium onions, sautéed in a little oil
3 tablespoons grated Parmesan or Cheddar cheese
1 cup thin white sauce, with a little tomato sauce added
Seasoning to taste

Cut cauliflower into small flowerets and boil, covered, in a little water until nearly done. Reserve water. Cover bottom of a Pyrex dish with the cooked onions, arrange cauliflower over them. Make white sauce, using the water in which cauliflower was boiled. Add tomato sauce to taste. Pour over cauliflower, sprinkle with cheese and dot with butter. Bake in 375 oven for 20-30 minutes. Serves 4-6.

Soya Bean Milk:

¾ cup soya beans, soaked overnight
2 cups water
1 teaspoon salt
1½ tablespoons brown sugar
3 cups water

Discussion of Diet and Recipes

In an electric blender, combine the soaked beans with 2 cups of water and blend at medium speed for 2 minutes. Pour into saucepan; add salt and brown sugar; bring to a boil, stirring constantly, and simmer for about 2 minutes. Strain, reserving residue. Return residue to saucepan, add 3 more cups of water, and repeat the process. Strain again and add this second batch of liquid to the first. If too thick, dilute with a little water. Keep in refrigerator. Shake before using. Yield, 5 cups.

Spinach Soufflé:

2 packages spinach
1 or 2 tablespoons dry mushrooms, soaked in water for ½ hour or an equivalent amount of fresh mushrooms
2 eggs, separated
3 tablespoons grated cheese
½ cup hot milk
Seasoning to taste
Dash of nutmeg
1 clove garlic, finely chopped
Soya oil

Boil spinach, drain well and chop coarsely. Combine egg yolks with milk, taking care not to curdle, and cook over very slow fire, stirring constantly, until mixture begins to thicken. Add to spinach. Season to taste with salt and nutmeg.

Cut up mushrooms and sauté in soya oil with the chopped garlic for 5-10 minutes. Add to spinach. Whip egg whites very stiff and fold into the mixture. Pour into casserole and bake in 375° oven for about 30 minutes. Serves 4-6.

Mushroom Sauce:

½ lb. fresh mushrooms *or* 1½ ounces dry mushrooms
1 tablespoon cooking oil
1 medium onion, finely chopped
1 clove garlic, finely chopped
Salt and pepper to taste
Sour cream to taste
Chopped parsley for garnish

If dry mushrooms are used, soak in water to cover for half an hour. Reserve water. Chop mushrooms but do not peel. Sauté onion and garlic in oil until transparent, add mushrooms and continue cooking over low flame, covered, until mushrooms are limp—about 10 minutes. Add a little of the water in which mushrooms have soaked to make a sauce. Season to taste, add sour cream and let bubble up. Simmer another 5-6 minutes. Add fresh parsley last.

Sauerkraut Salad:

1 lb. fresh sauerkraut
1 medium apple, diced
1 small onion, finely chopped
1 heaping tablespoon caraway seeds
2-3 tablespoons cooking oil
1 teaspoon honey

Sprinkle sauerkraut with caraway seeds. Add oil and honey, mix thoroughly and let stand at least half an hour, so that seeds will soften. Add chopped apple, mix again and serve. 4-6 servings.

Carrot-Rice-Nut Loaf:

4 whole eggs, lightly beaten
5 tablespoons vegetable oil
1 teaspoon vegetable salt
3 cups grated carrots
2 cups cooked brown rice
2 cups chopped walnuts
1 medium onion, chopped
1 green pepper, chopped (optional)

Combine eggs, oil and salt until thoroughly blended. Add other ingredients and mix thoroughly. Pour into lightly-greased casserole, press down lightly, and bake in 375° oven for 30 minutes. Serves 6.

Eggplant Steaks:

1 large eggplant, cut into ½-inch slices

Discussion of Diet and Recipes

Salt and pepper to taste
Butter

Season eggplant slices, dot each with butter and arrange in broiler. Broil under medium flame until tender. Serves 4.

Spinach and Rice Ring:

2 packages spinach, cooked and chopped
¼ cup milk
2 whole eggs, lightly beaten
1½ cups cooked brown rice
1 small onion, grated
Dash of nutmeg (optional)
Seasoning to taste

Mix all ingredients together, adding milk and beaten egg last. Bake in 400° oven for 30 minutes. Serves 4.

Appendix II

LETTERS TO THE AUTHOR

PUBLISHER'S NOTE: The following are but a few of the letters in praise of Indra Devi's popular and effective method of teaching Yoga, and in appreciation of her first book, *Forever Young, Forever Healthy*.[1]

Tel Aviv, Israel

Dear Indra Devi:

There are no words to tell you what Yoga has done for us. I simply do not know what would have happened to us without it, for it has brought not only happiness but an entirely new existence.

The Headstand and other exercises actually saved my husband's life when he was suffering a severe form of nervous depression and was on the verge of suicide.

I am unspeakably happy to have had the chance to study Yoga with you. My husband and I are able to teach it to other people and help them. Both of us and our students are eagerly awaiting the publication of your new book.

With all best wishes,
Ever gratefully,

Raya Riskin

---

[1] Englewood Cliffs, N.J.: Prentice-Hall, Inc., 1953.

Chicago

Dear Indra:

I am so deeply grateful for the exercises you taught me.

I wish that I were more faithful in doing them. I regularly do some of them, but alas, not all. Time seems always to plot against me. But the pain in my back has gone, and I feel so much better.

Devotedly,

Ellen Carpenter

Tarrytown, New York

Dear Madam Devi:

This is just a line to let you know how much I have enjoyed your book *Forever Young, Forever Healthy*. It agrees in every respect with our own philosophy of life. I have studied Yoga before, but never realized the importance of the various headstands and exercises—being a barbell fan myself. However, I am adding your exercises to the barbell and must say they are tremendous.

As you say, they are not for the mollycoddled who are too lazy and have too much lead in their system to go to the trouble of doing them. They have only themselves to blame for a feeble, senile, foggy-brained old age and plenty of doctor's bills.

Yours truly,

Robert G. Collier

New York City

Dearest Teacher:

Yoga does not need me to enhance its value, except for those who think that miracles do happen without effort and faith.

As you know, X-rays of my spine showed several calcium deposits. They were caused by two severe automobile accidents and a fall which aggravated my shocked condition, making an abdominal operation necessary.

Yoga exercises under you, plus my conscientious continuance of them at home, completely healed not only the spine but also all traces of scars. I recovered full use of the intestinal tract together with the natural functions of muscles atrophied by adhesions formed after operations.

Full coordination and use of movements in the dance have been restored naturally. With bodily health, my creative energies have been channeled into a new field—I started clay modeling for my own enjoyment and am already exhibiting now.

My own father-in-law, who is a doctor, was delighted at my finding a true teacher of Yoga who impressed me into never giving up its practice since it would keep me always in good health.

As ever,

Manuella

Brooklyn

Dear Miss Devi:

It was a great pleasure to meet you and to have you lecture at the Brooklyn Lodge of the Theosophical Society.

After hearing your lecture and seeing you demonstrate some of the genuine Yoga exercises, I decided to join one of your classes. I am thankful that I did so. The benefits, in such a short time, have been many. I had been suffering for several years from constipation of a most stubborn nature, exaggerated perhaps by the menopause. After the first exercises on Monday, I had real relief. To my surprise, a headache which had been bothering me for some ten days disappeared immediately after the first set of exercises that same day.

That evening I fell asleep much more quickly than I had in many months. I slept well all that night and felt well and strong the next day. These benefits have continued with the extra good fortune of getting rid of seventy-five per cent of the hot flashes and profuse perspiration day and night which had been destroying my health and disposition for over four years! I have had four lessons to date, and each week after attending your classes the defects just mentioned disappear more and more. I intend to follow the course until I am one hundred per cent healed!

What I have accomplished with your assistance during these few weeks is nothing short of miraculous! My nights were nightmarish with so many flashes and dripping perspiration winter and summer. During the day, my work exhausted me. Now all this has changed. I am being transformed day by day, it seems, thanks to you.

With kindest wishes and greetings to you, I am,

Sincerely,

Mrs. Maria F. Willis

Post Office, Entumeni
Zululand, South Africa

My dear Madam Devi:

Not so long ago, I came across your article on deep breathing . . . whereupon I immediately ordered your book. Its clear, simple and intelligent approach to Yoga impressed me so much that it prompted me to write you. I decided to order a supply so that people could get their copy without too much delay. It may please you to know that you have already acquired many ardent followers here in South Africa.

I am so thankful to say that the dull pain at my left side, in the kidney region, has subsided, and I feel so much better for doing the rhythmic breathing exercises for a few minutes twice daily. I am timing them to my walking pace when going to my office (I am an engineer here and live within walking distance). I have found that my eyesight is better although I have been taking the exercises for only eleven weeks.

Let me congratulate you and thank you for writing such a splendid and useful book. It has become a textbook for most Yoga teachers here.

Yours sincerely,

Cecil F. Wickes

Hollywood

Dear Indra:

After reading Smith's, Koussevitsky's, and St. Denis' letters in your book *Forever Young, Forever Healthy*, I felt like expressing my gratitude in writing, too. Your classes have changed my outlook on life so completely that I anxiously await each new glorious day with enthusiasm and optimism. I enjoy your classes so much because they have given me a sense of confidence, poise, peace, and contentment within my body, mind, and spirit which was unknown before or which was believed impossible of achieving. My meals taste better and digest better, my daily work goes more smoothly with fewer mistakes and frustrations, my ability in sports shows improvement, sickness rarely keeps me from my work or causes me expense, new opportunities for success seem to be opening up all around me, and successful people seem to be drawn into my acquaintance who are helping me and whom I am helping by bringing them to your wonderful classes. What I like most about your breathing exercises and postures is that: they are so simple and easily done once learned; they can be done at home or while traveling, either indoors or out, without complicated equipment, charts or expensive apparatus of any kind; they provide well-rounded daily exercise of the entire body as well as the mind and give you a feeling of determination and confidence in life.

My father, Bernarr Macfadden, who has studied exercise, diet, meditation, and fasting for fifty years . . . praises very highly the knowledge of body, mind, and spirit that you are teaching.

Most respectfully yours,

Jack Macfadden

Los Angeles

Dear Madame Indra Devi:

I am pleased to know of the plan for continuance of your classes which will beyond doubt prove beneficial to all participants as it has done for me.

It is with deep humility and gratitude that I take this opportunity to personally acknowledge the valuable effects of your high consciousness and splendid instruction of Yoga exercises.

Just a little more than three years ago it became necessary for me to undergo an operation for the removal of a tumor on the colon and intestinal tract. In the course of the operation the nerves in that region had to be severed, depriving me of natural elimination.

About two weeks after joining your classes and following the exercising instructions, I began to enjoy natural elimination again and I am happy to report that this condition has steadily improved.

I am indeed thankful beyond expression for the Divine guidance and wisdom which led me to you.

Very sincerely,

Ben Wiener

Ennis, Texas

Dear Miss Devi:

I am a Methodist minister, seventy-two years of age. I suffered from sciatic rheumatism several years ago, and it left a stiffness in my limbs, particularly my knees. I did not realize how great the stiffness was until I began your exercises. But, best of all, I never knew what complete relief was until I learned to relax the bones of the spine and pelvis through your Yoga exercises.

I began attempting to practice some of the simpler ones and to my amazement just a few minutes spent at them seemed to give me a wonderful "lift" both physically and mentally.

I am really convinced of the merits of this system, and intend to do the exercises more regularly.

My elimination is so much better, also the terrible bloating after meals, dizziness, etc. My general feeling of well-being has greatly improved thanks to you.

It is my sincere belief that if I had known and practiced the principles of Yoga many years ago, I could have enjoyed not only a higher degree of good health, but could have given better service to God and man. I should say that Yoga is proving that Occidentals have much to learn from the Orientals who have steadfastly practiced these health-building principles for hundreds of years.

With kindest regards to you and sincere appreciation of the service you are rendering to suffering people.

I am gratefully yours,

Roy A. Langston
Pastor, First Methodist Church

P.S. I have a friend who had the same troubles as I. He bought your book a week later and reports similar favorable results.

Letters to the Author

St. Petersburg, Florida

Dear Miss Devi:

I became afflicted with rheumatoid arthritis at the age of seventeen and in a matter of months was helpless in bed with every joint of my body ankylosed. After 6 years the doctors gave me up and my parents brought me to Florida.

Recently our neighbors introduced me to Yoga and in particular to your wonderful book, *Forever Young, Forever Healthy*.

On August 1st of this year I started on the sixty-day lemon juice plan and also the lemon and orange leaves tea (it is delicious) as outlined in your book. I am unable to do the Yoga postures but another son of the same neighbor works with me every day, practicing the movements I *can* make. The results have been remarkable. I am developing muscles and strength, have increased mobility, particularly in the hips and spine which have been so tight. The shoulders, arms, and ankles are also looser. I am now able to take full steps forward (with assistance), and since last week also backward. With the help of my friends or my parents I go swimming every other day in the Gulf where I also exercise. I can walk, although stiff-kneed, swim and float alone. I am doing the deep breathing and following your diet-suggestion and have faith in recovering fully.

Thank you so much for taking the time to read this letter, and I thank you from my heart and soul.

Sincerely,

Thelma L.

APPENDIX II

New York City

Dear Madam Devi:

I was one of your students in your New York classes, and want to wish you every happiness.

I cannot thank you enough for helping me to get rid of the constipation from which I have suffered for 30 years.

Thanks to you, I am reborn.

God bless you always,

Sincerely,

Helen C.

Belle Glade, Florida

Dear Indra Devi:

Many of my friends here were amazed at the recovery I made and some of them immediately became very interested in Yoga.

They knew that I had a bad case of bronchitis and arthritis and they are surprised to see me free of these troubles.

I have also suffered from a fallen womb for 15 years and, since taking your Yoga exercises, this condition has been completely adjusted.

With everlasting gratitude for your help,

Sincerely yours,

Frances C. Leifer

Letters to the Author

Bombay, India

Dear Shrimati Indra Devi,

You, no doubt, already know the good news that the Sindhi translation of your book has received an award from our Government—we all are very happy and proud of you.

Your book has made even us Indians more keenly aware of the great benefits of the Yoga Asanas—you have rendered a great service to humanity by writing it. You would be surprised to know how many people here have benefited by following your instructions. One of our close friends, for example, the wife of a University professor, suffered for many years from nervous stomach troubles, arthritis, and female disorders. After a few months of Yoga practice and following your diet, she has completely recovered from all her troubles and feels a different person now.

Books are my hobby: you know that I am the first man to have published in pictures our sacred Bhagavat Gita. Allow me to congratulate and thank you for having written such a precious and useful book.

Your sincere friend,

Parmanand S. Mehra

Houston, Texas

Dear Miss Devi:

May I extend my heart-felt and deepest good thoughts for you and your work?

I am thirty years old, and a professional musician. I have also been an alcoholic for eleven years.

Since practicing the Yoga postures diligently for the past few months, following the diet you outlined in your book, and sleeping on a hard surface, I have achieved the following results:

(1) I have given up liquor and no longer have any desire for it.
(2) I have also lost interest in smoking, soft drinks, and spicy foods —something I never dreamed possible.
(3) I have lost much of my excess weight, am less nervous and depressed.
(4) There have been remarkable improvements in my health; my liver condition and my ulcerative colitis are much better.

My friends are amazed at the changes Yoga has brought about in me. I want to continue progress in this wonderful gift to mankind, and would like to help others some day.

Thank you, and may the Higher Self smile on you forever.

T. N.

Osaka, Japan

Letters to the Author

Dear Miss Devi:

I have your book *Forever Young, Forever Healthy*, translated into Japanese, and am very pleased with it.

I am thirty-eight years old and have suffered great pains due to a nervous heart condition. Since I started on the Yoga postures, my pains have decreased greatly. My wife, thirty-two years old, has found the exercises of much help in losing weight, and my five-year-old son has no more asthma trouble since the day he began exercising. I also have a daughter, ten, and both children have had a lot of trouble with tonsilitis, but, thanks to the Lion Posture, their sore throats are much better. Our family has found the Yoga exercises very useful for promoting better elimination.

You, through your book, have given us a new way of life. We sincerely hope to join your class when you come to Osaka.

Yours very truly,
R. T.

Bad Homburg, Germany

Much esteemed Miss Indra Devi:

Your kind letter arrived on Christmas day and I must tell you that it was my best Christmas present.

I am so glad that you have decided to write another book and to include in it suggestions for concentration and meditation.

You are such a good teacher that it is almost impossible to make a mistake when following your instructions.

Personally, I am of the opinion that your book is the best one on Yoga. I have read a number of them but none is as clear and applicable as yours.

I want to report to you that we all are working diligently and I am making steady progress with the Lotus Pose and other postures, but I am not 100% good as yet. The Headstand is priceless and the results thereof most outstanding. The Yoga exercises are remarkable: The fat ones get slimmer and the thin ones gain weight and get stronger; constipation disappears, the body becomes elastic and the spirits brighten up.

I am a seeker and you have given me so much.

Wishing you every thing good,

I am always at your service,

A. G.

Merrickville,
Ontario, Canada

Miss Indra Devi:

I have one of your books, *Forever Young, Forever Healthy.*

I think it is the most wonderful book ever printed. I have suffered for twenty-five years and I am getting better. If I can do as you say I will be well again soon. I have wanted to write you and tell you about it.

I hope you will write more books, I would like to see one in every home.

Sincerely,

William B.

Philadelphia

Dear Miss Devi:

For one week I have had in my possession your wonderful book, *Forever Young, Forever Healthy.* I have enjoyed every bit of it.

Now I am writing to let you know how much, in this short time, the exercises have done for me. I feel happier, I am sure my waist is smaller and my eating habits are changed.

Yoga has always appealed to me and I was surprised that there was such a wonderful book.

It will be very interesting for me to see how I come out after about six months of your exercises.

I am forty-six and don't refute my years and I was happy to see that you don't wish for your youth again, either.

Sincerely,

(Mrs.) K. S.

Hollywood

Dearest Indra Devi:

What did I do before Yoga! As you know I spent thirteen months in bed. During this time I gained weight and my muscles became soft and lost their tone. Yoga was the answer for me. I lost my excess weight gradually, at the same time firming my flabby muscles. The deep breathing seemed to help appease my appetite so that I was satisfied with less food.

But the greatest benefit of all, I believe, is the sense of peace and poise which developed within me. I no longer feel overwhelmed by hectic situations, nor pressed for time.

My husband too has experienced wonderful results. Some years ago he suffered a brain concussion. This left him with a certain dizziness whenever he turned his head or made a sudden movement. The doctors told him that this was the result of a permanent damage to that part of the brain which controls balance. However, this has completely disappeared since he has been practicing Yoga.

Also, his back was quite painful and he required a pillow to support it for the past twenty years. Now, no more trouble!

As a "bonus," my husband who was losing his hair, discovered that he no longer finds any hair in his brush or comb. We both feel that the Headstand is responsible for this.

I can't tell you what it has meant to have such an excellent teacher. Bless you!

Most sincerely,

Martha Strauss

Letters to the Author

Vancouver

Dear Miss Devi:

Thank you for your most interesting book, *Forever Young, Forever Healthy*, which you sent me with your autograph.

Also, I take this opportunity to express anew my gratitude for the wonderful help I derived years ago, in China, when I was ready to be operated on for sinus trouble. You suggested, then, to try the Headstand. After four months, the sinus condition had cleared up, to the great surprise of my doctor. It never recurred.

With my heartfelt thanks,

Sincerely yours,

Therese Voelker

Los Angeles

Dear Indra Devi:

After the first day of doing the exercises from your interesting book, *Forever Young, Forever Healthy*, I was convinced that this series of exercises was out of this world.

Gratefully,

Lillian McGovern

Index

Abdominal fat, exercises for reduction of:
  Bending-Forward posture, 54-55
  Body-Raising pose, 53-54
  Footlift pose, 55-57, 98-99, 123
  Raised-Legs posture, 19-21
  Stretching posture, 91-93
  Swan posture, 114-116
  Wood-Chopping movement, 148
Abdominal Lift, 118-121
  benefits of, 119-120
  caution, 120
  (ill.), 119
  technique, 118
  time, 118-119
  variation of, 120-121
Abdominal muscles, exercises for strengthening:
  Abdominal Lift, 118-121
  Body-Raising pose, 53-54
  Churning pose, 121-123
  Raised-Legs posture, 19-21
  Yoga Mudra, 50-53
Accomplished pose, 64-66
  (ill.), 65
  technique, 66
Adrenal glands:
  exercises beneficial for:
    Cobra pose, 27-29
    Supine pose, 145-147
    Twist posture, 116-118, 142-143, 163-165
  function of, 107
  location of, 107
Ajna chakra, 132
Albin, Carl, 83

Alcohol, 78, 80
All, communion with, 4-5
Alsaker, Rasmus, 1
Anahat chakra, 132
Angular Balance pose, 162-163
  (ill.), 163
  technique, 162
  time, 162
Angular Rest pose, 161-162
  benefits of, 162
  (ill.), 162
  technique, 161
  time, 161
Animals, learning from behavior of, 4
Ankles, strengthening, exercises for, 124-126, 167-168
Arches, fallen, exercise for, 124-126
Ardha-baddha-pada-uttānasana, 55-57, 98-99, 123
Ardha Matsyendrāsana, 116-118, 142-143, 163-165
Arms, exercises for strengthening, 114-116, 167-168
Arohanāsana, 53-54
Arthritis, relief of:
  exercises:
    Angular Rest pose, 161-162
    Plough posture, 93-94
  through potato preparations, 188
Asanas, 9 (*see also* Postures)
  Ardha-baddha-pada-uttānasana, 55-57, 98-99, 123
  Ardha Matsyendrāsana, 116-118, 142-143, 163-165
  Arohanāsana, 53-54
  basic, 27

215

Asanas (Cont.):
  Bhujangāsana, 27-29
  Halāsana, 93-94
  Hastapadāsana, 54-55
  Janushirshāsana, 21-23
  Nauli, 121-123
  number of existing, 160
  Oopavishta-Konāsana, 141-142
  Padmāsana, 9, 23-27
  Parvatāsana, 165-167
  Paschimatanāsana, 91-93
  purpose of, 57
  Samāsana, 9, 66
  Saroangāsana, 143-145
  Shirshana, 85-91, 105-106, 112-114, 137-141, 160-161
  Siddhāsana, 9, 64-66
  Simhāsana, 96-98
  Soopta-Konāsana, 161-162
  Swanāsana, 114-116
  Swastikāsana, 9, 66
  Udhitta Padāsana, 19-21
  Ustrāsana, 95-96
  Utkāsana, 29-32
Asthma, exercises for:
  Angular Rest pose, 161-162
  breathing, 32
  Headstand, 85-91, 112-114, 137-141
  Shoulderstand, 143-145
  Supine pose, 145-147
  Twist posture, 116-118, 142-143, 163-165
Astral body, 128
  Chakras, 130-132
  nadis, 128-130
Awareness:
  defined, 174
  facets of, 174-175

Back, strengthening, exercises for:
  Body-Raising pose, 53-54
  breathing, 59-63
  Swan posture, 114-116
  Twist posture, 116-118, 142-143, 163-165
Backache, overcoming, exercises for:
  breathing exercise, 32-33
  Cobra pose, 27-29
Balanced Nutrition—Know What You Eat and Why, Pfeiffer, 73
Balance exercises:
  Angular Balance pose, 162-163

Balance exercises *(Cont.):*
  breathing, 124-126
  Footlift, 55-57, 98-99, 123
Bandha, 27
Banik, Allen E., 77
Bending-Forward posture, 54-55
  benefits of, 54
  caution, 54-55
  (ill.), 55
  techniques, 54
  time, 54
Bhujangāsana, 27-29
Blood circulation, improving through exercise:
  Angular Rest pose, 161-162
  Headstand, 85-91, 112-114, 137-141
  Shoulderstand, 143-145
Blood vessel diseases and diet, 70-71
Body:
  astral, 128-132
  occult center of, 130
Body Chemistry in Health and Disease, Page, 75
Body heat, development of through exercise, 27-29
Body-Raising pose, 53-54
  benefits, 53-54
  caution, 54
  (ill.), 53
  technique, 53
  time, 53
Boone, J. Allen, 151
Brahmacharin, 153
Brain, need for oxygen, 39
Breathing:
  anatomy of, 6-7
  deep, 4-12
    importance of for smokers, 41
    incorrect, 40
    raising I.Q. by, 40
  effects of, 38-44
    on mental health, 39-40
    on metabolism, 40-41
  function of, 38-39
  importance of to life, 38-39
  and old age, 42
  ordinary deep, 6
  ordinary unconscious, 5
  rhythmic, 11, 43, 63-64
  during sleep, 7-8
  Yoga deep:
    benefits of, 9
    compared with ordinary deep, 6

Index

Breathing *(Cont.)*:
  described, 8
  exhalation, 8, 10-11
  inhalation, 8, 10
  learning, 7-8, 10-11
  overdoing, results of, 11
Breathing exercises:
  for asthma sufferers, 32
  for balance, 124-126
  Cleansing Breath, 99-100
  for good posture, 59-63
  lesson's final, 126
    (ill.), 127
  Mountain pose, 165-167
    (ill.), 166
  poses for, 9
    Accomplished *(Siddhāsana)*, 64-66
    Lotus *(Padmāsana)*, 23-27
    Swastikāsana, 66
    Symmetrical *(Samāsana)*, 66
  push-ups, 167-168
    benefits of, 168
    against wall *(ill.)*, 167
  recharging breath, 147
  for relief of "morning" backache, 32-33
  for relief of sacroiliac troubles, 32-33
  rhythmic:
    benefits of, 63
    technique, 63-64
    time, 64
  for stronger calves and ankles, 124-126
  Walking Breathing, 100-101
  wood-chopping movement, 148
    (ill.), 149
  Yoga, suitability of for Westerners, 43-44
Buddha pose, 27
Buddhist Commandments, 152
Building for Mental and Physical Health, Rice, 40
Bust muscles, strengthening exercise, 167-168

Calcium Cocktail, 82-83
Calves, strengthening exercises for, 124-126, 167-168
Camel posture, 95-96
  benefits of, 96
  caution, 96
  (ill.), 95

Camel posture *(Cont.)*:
  technique, 95
  time, 95-96
Cancer:
  linked to oxygen starvation, 41-42
  linked to poor diet, 69
  and smoking, 41
Cancer Therapy, The, Gerson, 69
"Candle" pose, 143
Carbohydrates:
  in diet, 73, 81-82
  digestion of, 182
Carrington, Hereward, 133
Celibacy, 153
Chakras, 130-132
  (chart), 131
  defined, 130
Changing vision exercise, 16
Chela, 153
Chest, strengthening exercises, 114-116, 167-168
Chocolate, 80
Cholesterol, 71, 82
Christ, 135
Churning pose, 121-123
  benefits of, 123
  caution, 123
  (ill.), 122
  technique, 121
Clairvoyance, seat of, 132
Clauson, Chris, 69
Cleanliness, internal, 36-37, 42, 120
Cleansing Breath, 99-100
Cleansing diet, 185
Clothing:
  for exercises, 4
  during sleep, 38
Cobra pose, 27-29
  benefits of, 28-29
  caution, 29
  (ill.), 28
  technique, 27-28
  time, 28
Cocoa, 80
Coffee, 80
Coffee enema, 37
Commentaries on Living, Krishnamurti, 154, 174
Concentration:
  on abstract matters, 179
  choosing objects for, 177, 178-179
  defined, 169

Concentration *(Cont.)*:
  mastering, effect of on personality, 172
  vs. meditation, 169
  positive and negative use of, 173-174
  practice of, 176-178
  teaching children, 172-173
  thought-prejection, 173
Concentration and Meditation, Paramanada, 67, 169, 176
Concentration poses *(see* Meditative poses)
Constipation:
  enemas, 32
  exercises for relief of:
    Abdominal Lift, 118-121
    Angular Rest pose, 161-162
    Bending-Forward posture, 54-55
    Body-Raising pose, 53-54
    Camel posture, 95-96
    Churning pose, 121-123
    Footlift pose, 55-57, 98-99, 123
    Headstand, 85-91, 112-114, 137-141
    Head-to-Knee posture, 21-23
    Plough posture, 93-94
    Shoulderstand, 143-145
    Squatting pose, 29-32
    Stretching posture, 91-93
    Twist posture, 116-118, 142-143, 163-165
    Yoga Mudra, 50-53
  and faulty diet, 72
Contemplation, 153-157
Cosmic Energy, centers of, 130
Coudry, E. Vincent, 69

Darshana, Yoga, 111
Dental health, 36, 75, 76
Diet, 67-84, 181-189
  and age, 72-73
  after age sixty, 187
  after age thirty-five, 187-188
  author's, 181-182
  bleached foods, 74
  Calcium Cocktail, 82-83
  cleansing, 185
  "dead" foods, 74
  and dental health, 75, 76
  detrimental food combinations, 182
  fats, 70-71, 82
  flour, 74, 75-76
  fried foods, 81-82
  fruit vs. fruit juices, 80

Diet *(Cont.)*:
  Hay Diet, 182
  food classification *(table)*, 183-184
  health, 185-186
  honey in, 74-75
  individual needs, 72-73
  juice, 74
    cabbage, 82
    enzymes in, 69, 80
    vs. fruit, 80
    vegetable, preparing, 80
  meat, 74, 78-79, 185
  mental attitude toward, 83-84
  milk, 71, 80
  and morphology, 72
  "musts" of, 73
  natural, benefits of, 76-77
  poor, and diseases, 67-72
    blood vessels, 70-71
    cancer, 69
    gallstones, 68-69
    heart, 70-71
    indigestion, 72
    kidney, 71
    liver, 71
    mental illness, 68
    polio, 75
  processed foods, 74
  protein in, 73, 83, 182, 183-184
  raw foods, 74
  recipes, 189-195
  reducing, 186-187
  refined foods, 74
  starch in, 73, 81, 182, 183-184
  stimulants in, 78, 80
  sugar, 74-75
  suggestions for healthy, 79-83
  of teenagers, 70
  vegetables, 74, 77, 78, 81
  of Yoga disciples, 78
Diet Prevents Polio, Sandler, 75
Digestion, effect of oxygen on, 40-41
Diseases:
  linked to poor diet, 67-72
  psychosomatic origin of, 108-109, 170
Divine marriage of Spirit and Matter, 132-133
Durville, Gaston, 128-129

Education and the Significance of Life, Krishnamurti, 154
Eisenhower, Dwight D., 79

Index

Elimination, exercises for improvement of:
  Squatting pose, 29-32
  Swan posture, 114-116
Elwood, Catharyn, 76
Emerson, Ralph Waldo, 159
Emotional stress, effects of, 108-109, 170-171
Endocrine glands, 106-109
  function of, 107
  location of, 106-107
  system of *(chart)*, 106
Endocrinology, 129
Enemas, 37, 42, 46
Energy, increasing, exercises for:
  Bending-Forward posture, 54-55
  Headstand, 85-91, 112-114, 137-141
  Head-to-Knee posture, 21-23
  Recharging Breath, 147
  Wood-Chopping movement, 148
  defined, 69
  demonstration of, 70
Exercises:
  Abdominal Lift, 118-121
  adverse effects of at start, 45-46
  Angular Balance pose, 162-163
  Angular Rest pose, 161-162
  avoiding mistakes in, 111-112
  basic Yoga, 27
  Bending-Forward posture, 54-55
  Body-Raising pose, 53-54
  breathing *(see* Breathing)
  Camel posture, 95-96
  changing-vision, 16
  Churning pose, 121-123
  clothing for, 4
  Cobra pose, 27-29
  conditions for, 4
  eye, 14-16
  Footlift pose, 55-57, 98-99, 123
  general rules for, 36, 111-112
  in group, 159
  Half-Headstand, 48-50
  Headstand, 27, 85-91, 105-106, 112-114, 137-141, 160-161
  Head-to-Knee posture, 21-23
  leg stretching, 3, 47
  Lion posture, 96-98
  Mountain pose, 165-167
  neck, 12-14
  palming, 16
  Plough posture, 27, 93-94
  Raised-Legs posture, 19-21

Exercises *(Cont.):*
  Reverse posture, 57-59
  rocking, 17-19
  schedule for, 2, 47, 159-161
  Shoulderstand, 27, 143-145
  Squatting pose, 29-32
  Stoop, 50-53
  Stretching posture, 27, 91-93
  Supine pose, 145-147
  Swan posture, 114-116
  Triangle pose, 141-142
  Twist posture, 27, 116-118, 142-143, 163-165
  Wood-chopping movement, 148-149
  Yoga Mudra, 50-53
Eye exercises, 14-16
  technique, 15-16
Eye troubles, relief of through Headstand, 90

Fatigue, exercise for overcoming, 85-91, 112-114, 137-141
Fats in diet, 70-71, 82
Fear, overcoming, exercise for, 85-91, 112-114, 137-141
Feel Like a Million, Elwood, 76
Female disorders, exercises for:
  Angular Rest pose, 161-162
  Camel posture, 95-96
  Churning pose, 121-123
  Cobra pose, 27-29
  Headstand, 85-91, 112-114, 137-141
  Reverse posture, 57-59
  Shoulderstand, 143-145
Fertilizers, organic vs. chemical, 69-70, 77
First and Last Freedom, The Krishnamurti, 154
Fish posture, 145, 161
Flour, bleached, 74, 75-76
Flowers in bedroom, 37
Fluid intake, 42, 80
Food *(see* Diet)
Footlift pose:
  benefits of, 99
  first movement, 55-57
  (ill.), 56
  technique, 55-56
  second movement, 98-99
  (ill.), 98
  technique, 98-99
  time, 99

Footlift pose *(Cont.)*:
  third movement, 123
  (ill.), 124
Forearms, exercises for slimming and strengthening, 167-168
Forever Young, Forever Healthy, Devi, 43

Gallstones linked to poor diet, 68-69
Gas pains:
  and diet, 81
  exercises recommended for:
    Abdominal Lift, 118-121
    Bending-Forward posture, 54-55
    Cobra pose, 27-29
    Camel posture, 95-96
    Footlift pose, 55-57, 98-99, 123
  food combinations causing, 182
Gautama, 135
Gerson, Max, 69
Glands *(see* Adrenal, Endocrine, Parathyroid, Pineal, Pituitary, Sex, Thymus and Thyroid glands)
Gonads *(see* Sex glands)
Guru, 128

Halāsana, 93-94
Half-Headstand, 48-50
  caution, 50
  (ill.), 49
  technique, 48-50
Hastapadāsana, 54-55
Hay, William Howard, 182
Hay diet, 182
  food classification *(table)*, 183-184
Headaches, exercise for, 85-91, 112-114, 137-141
Headstand, 27, 160-161
  benefits of, 90
  caution, 90-91
  in corner, 85-91
  (ills.), 86, 87
  technique, 88-89
  time, 89
  effects of, 105-106
  free, 137-141
    (ills.), 138, 140
    technique, 137-139
    time, 140-141
  half *(see* Half-Headstand)
  against wall, 112-114
    (ill.), 113
    technique, 112-114

Headstand *(Cont.)*:
  against wall *(Cont.)*:
    time, 114
Head-to-Knee posture, 21-23
  benefits of, 21
  (ill.), 22
  technique, 21
  time, 21
Health diet, 185-186
Heart diseases and animal fat diet, 70-71
High Enema Without Apparatus, The, McFerrin, 120
Higher Psychical Development, Carrington, 133
Honey:
  in diet, 74-75
  enema, 37
Hormones, *defined*, 107
How to Live 365 Days a Year, Schindler, 107, 170
Human Destiny, Lecomte Du Noüy, 67
Hunza-Land, The, Banik, 77
Iced water, 79
Ida, 130
Illness:
  linked to poor diet, 67-72
  psychosomatic origin of, 108-109, 170
  resuming exercises after, 36
Indigestion:
  exercises for relief of:
    Abdominal Lift, 118-121
    Angular Rest pose, 161-162
    Churning pose, 121-123
    Head-to-Knee posture, 21-23
    Plough posture, 93-94
    Stretching posture, 91-93
    Twist posture, 116-118, 142-143, 163-165
  and faulty diet, 72
  food combinations causing, 182
Insomnia, overcoming, exercises for:
  Headstand, 85-91, 112-114, 137-141
  rocking, 17-19
Internal cleanliness, 36-37, 42, 120
Intestines, exercise for strengthening, 145-147
Introspection, 153-157
I.Q., effect of breathing on, 40

Jacobson, Max, 40
Janushirshāsana, 21-23

Index

Juice, in diet, 74
  cabbage, 82
  enzymes in, 69, 80
  vegetable, preparing, 80
  vs. whole fruit, 80
Juvenile delinquency, 40

Kidney degeneration, and diet, 71
Kidneys, exercises for:
  Churning pose, 121-123
  Supine pose, 145-147
  Twist posture, 116-118, 142-143, 163-165
Kinship with All Life, Boone, 151
Knauer, Sigfrid, 150
Knees, relieving stiffness in, 29-31
Knowledge of self, 153-157
Krishna, Bala, 65
Krishnaji (*see* Krishnamurti, Jiddu)
Krishnamachrya, Sri, 160
Krishnamurti, Jiddu, 154, 155, 174
Kundalini power, 128-135
  ascending, 132-133
  connection of with sex energy, 133-134
  and Genesis legend, 133
  symbolism, 130-131

Lancelin, Charles, 128-129
Legs, strengthening, exercises for:
  breathing exercise, 124-126
  Footlift posture, 55-57, 98-99, 123
  Head-to-Knee posture, 21-23
Leg stretching exercise, 3, 47
Lion posture, 96-98
  benefits of, 96, 97
  caution, 98
  (*ill.*), 97
  technique, 96-97
  time, 97
Liver, exercises for:
  Abdominal Lift, 118-121
  Angular Rest pose, 161-162
  Churning pose, 121-123
  Headstand, 85-91, 112-114, 137-141
  Plough posture, 93-94
  Twist posture, 116-118, 142-143, 163-165
Liver degeneration, and diet, 71
Loehr, Franklin, 173
Los Angeles *Examiner*, 69
Los Angeles *Times*, 68, 71, 75

Lotus pose, 9, 23-27
  described, 24-26
  (*ill.*), 24
  practice for, 23-24
  (*ill.*), 25
  preliminary exercise, 23
  use of in India, 27
Lumbago, exercises for relief of:
  Squatting pose, 29-32
  Stretching posture, 91-93
Lungs, cleansing exercise for, 99-100

McFerrin, Charles B., 120
Manipura chakra, 132
Mattress, 3, 38
Meat, 74, 78-79, 185
Meditation, 34-35, 153-157
  on abstract matters, 179
  vs. concentration, 169
  defined, 169, 175
  practice of, 178
  vs. prayer, 175
Meditative poses, 9
  Accomplished (*Siddhāsana*), 64-66
  Lotus (*Padmāsana*), 23-27
  Swastikāsana, 66
  Symmetrical (*Samāsana*), 66
Memory, exercise for improvement of, 85-91, 112-114, 137-141
Menopause troubles, exercise for, 57-59
Menstruation, exercises during, 36
Menstruation troubles, exercises for:
  Angular Rest pose, 161-162
  Churning pose, 121-123
  Reverse posture, 57-59
  Shoulderstand, 143-145
Mental illness:
  caused by oxygen starvation, 39-40
  caused by poor diet, 68
Metabolic disorders, and diet, 70-71
Milk, 71, 80
Mohammed, 135
Morals, Yoga code of, 150
"Morning" backache, breathing exercise for, 32-33
Morning routine, 3-4, 47-48
Mountain pose, 165-167
  (*ills.*), 166
Mouth, hygiene of, 36
Mudras, 27
  purpose of, 57

Mudras (Cont.):
   Viparitakarani, 57-59
   Yoga Mudra, 50-53
Muenchener Illustrierte, 104
Muladhara chakra, 130-131
Muscular rheumatism, exercises for:
   Angular Rest pose, 161-162
   Plough posture, 93-94
Muscular tension, 102-104
   treatment of, 104-109

Nadis:
   defined, 128
   most important, 130
Nauli, 121-123
Neck, strengthening, exercise for, 145-147
Neck exercises, 12-14
   benefits of, 14
   technique, 13-14
   testing need for, 12-13
Nervousness, overcoming, exercise for, 85-91, 112-114, 137-141
Nervous system, exercises for:
   Angular Rest pose, 161-162
   Cobra pose, 27-29
   Rocking, 17-19
   Shoulderstand, 143-145
   Supine pose, 145-147
   Yoga Mudra, 50-53
Neuro-muscular tension, 102-104
   treatment of, 102-104
New England Journal of Medicine, The, 71
New Yorker, The, 109
Niyama, 150, 152-153
Nose troubles, relief of through Headstand, 90
Noüy, Lecomte Du, 67

Obesity, exercises for:
   Angular Rest pose, 161-162
   Plough posture, 93-94
   Twist posture, 116-118, 142-143, 163-165
Occult center of body, 130
Ojas, 134, 153
Old age, speeded by incorrect breathing, 42
Oopavishta-Konāsana, 141-142
Organs, keeping youthful, exercise for, 57-59 (*see also* Kidneys; Liver; Lungs; Pelvic organs; Stomach)

Ovarian troubles, exercises recommended for:
   Churning pose, 121-123
   Cobra pose, 27-29
Oxygen, importance of, 39-41
Oxygen, Master of Cancer, Totney, 41
Oxygen starvation:
   and aging process, 42
   effect on brain, 39-40
   effect on organs, 40
   as possible cause of cancer, 41-42
   results of, 41

Padmas, 130-132
   (chart), 131
   defined, 130
Padmāsana, 9, 23-27 (*see also* Lotus pose)
Page, Melvin E., 75
Palming exercise, 16
Pancreas troubles, exercise recommended for, 121-123
Paramananda, Swami, 67, 169, 176, 179
Parathyroid glands, 107
   exercise beneficial for, 85-91, 112-114, 137-141
Parvatāsana, 165-167
Paschimatanāsana, 91-93
Patanjali, 169
Payne, Eugene H., 71
Pelvic organs, exercises for:
   displacement, 95-96
   strengthening, 143-145, 161-162
   toning, 145-147
Pelvic region, strengthening, exercises for:
   Body-Raising pose, 53-54
   Stretching posture, 91-93
   Yoga Mudra, 50-53
Pfeiffer, Ehrenfried E., 17, 72, 73
Pharyngeal area, 6
Pineal gland, 106-107
   effect of Headstand on, 105-106
   exercises beneficial for:
      Headstand, 85-91, 112-114, 137-141
      Supine pose, 145-147
Pingala, 130
Pituitary gland, 90, 106-109
   effect of Headstand on, 105-106
   exercises beneficial for:
      Headstand, 85-91, 112-114, 137-141
      Supine pose, 145-147
   function of, 107

Index

Pituitary gland *(Cont.):*
  importance of, 107-108
  location of, 106-107
Plants in bedroom, 37
Plough posture, 27, 93-94
  benefits of, 94
  caution, 94
  (ill.), 93
  technique, 93-94
  time, 94
  variation of, 94
Polio, linked to sugar consumption, 75
Poses *(see* Postures)
Posture, good:
  exercises for:
    breathing, 59-63
    Twist posture, 116-118, 142-143, 163-165
  importance of, 9
Postures:
  Accomplished, 64-66
  Angular Balance, 162-163
  Angular Rest, 161-162
  avoiding mistakes in, 111-112
  basic Yoga, 27
  Bending-Forward, 54-55
  Body-Raising, 53-54
  Buddha pose, 27
  for breathing exercises, 9, 64-66
  Camel, 95-96
  Churning, 121-123
  Cobra, 27-29
  concentration, 9, 64-66
  Footlift, 55-57, 98-99, 123
  general rules, 111-112
  Half-Headstand, 48-50
  Headstand, 27, 85-91, 105-106, 112-114, 137-141, 160-161
  Head-to-Knee, 21-23
  health check before doing, 38
  Lion, 96-98
  Lotus pose, 9, 23-27
  meditative, 9, 64-66
  Mountain, 165-167
  Plough, 27, 93-94
  Raised-Legs, 19-21
  Reverse, 57-59
  Rocking exercise, 17-19
  Shoulderstand, 27, 143-145
  Squatting, 29-32
  Stretching, 27, 91-93
  Supine, 145-147
  Swan, 114-116

Postures *(Cont.):*
  Swastikāsana, 66
  Symmetrical, 66
  Triangle, 141-142
  Twist, 27, 116-118, 142-143, 163-165
Potency, exercise for preserving or regaining, 57-59 *(see also* Seminal weakness)
Power of Prayer on Plants, The, Loehr, 173
Powers, Mala, 164
Practical Guide for Students of Yoga, Sivananda, 175
Prana:
  circulation of in body, 128
  defined, 9, 44, 128
  knowledge of in antiquity, 129
  Western scientists' attitude toward, 129
Pranayama, 43, 129
Prayer vs. meditation, 175
Pregnancy:
  diet during, 70
  doing exercises during, 36
  exercise beneficial after, 143-145
Protein:
  digestion of, 182
  in diet, 73, 83
  foods containing, 183-184

Raised-Legs posture, 19-21
  benefits of, 20
  caution, 21
  (ill.), 20
  technique, 19-20
  time, 20
Reader's Digest, 70
Recharging breath, 147
Reducing diet, 186-187
Relaxation, 33-35, 102-105, 109
  through Headstand, 105-106
  through rhythmic breathing, 109
Reverse posture, 27, 57-59
  benefits of, 57-59
  (ills.), 58, 60
  technique, 57
  time, 57
Rheumatism, muscular, exercises for:
  Angular Rest pose, 161-162
  Plough posture, 93-94
Rhythmic breathing, 11, 43, 63-64
  benefits of, 63

Rhythmic breathing *(Cont.):*
  technique, 63-64
  time, 64
Rice, Philip, 39, 40
Rochat, Albert, 128-129
Rocking exercise, 17-19
  benefits of, 17, 19
  (ill.), 18
  scheduling, 47
  technique, 18
  time, 19
Romana, Jacques, 109

Sacroiliac troubles, relief of through breathing, 32-33
Sahasrara chakra, 132
St. Denis, Ruth, 143, 144
Samadhi, 132
Samāsana, 9, 66
Sandler, Benjamin F., 75
Sarvangāsana, 143-145
Savāsana, 33
Schedule for exercises, 2, 47, 159-161
Schindler, John A., 107, 170
Schoepfer, G. J., 71
Schweitzer, Albert, 151
Self, knowledge of, 153-157
Self-discipline, 157
Self-improvement, methods of, 174
Selye, Hans, 108
Seminal weakness, exercises for overcoming:
  Angular Rest pose, 161-162
  Shoulderstand, 143-145
  Yoga Mudra, 50-53
Serpent power *(see* Kundalini power)
Sex, Yoga attitude toward, 133-134, 153
Sex glands, 107
  exercises beneficial for:
    Angular Rest pose, 161-162
    Camel posture, 95-96
    Reverse posture, 57-59
    Shoulderstand, 143-145
  restoring balance and activity of, 83
Shirshāsana, 85-91, 105-106, 112-114, 137-141
Shoulders, strengthening, exercises for:
  Body-Raising pose, 53-54
  breathing, 59-63
  Swan posture, 114-116
  Twist posture, 116-118, 142-143, 163-165

Shoulderstand, 27, 143-145
  benefits of, 145
  caution, 145
  (ill.), 144
  technique, 144-145
Shushumna, 130
Siddhāsana, 9, 64-66
Silence, periods of, 155-157
Simhāsana, 96-98
Sivananda, Swami, 175
Skin, exercise for keeping youthful, 57-59
Sleep:
  breathing during, 7-8
  clothing for, 38
  getting up from, 3-4
  improving, exercises for:
    Headstand, 85-91, 112-114, 137-141
    rocking, 17-19
  mattress, 3, 38
  pillows, 38
  suggestions for, 37-38
Slouching, exercises for, 59-63, 114-118
Smoking, 41, 78, 79
Soopta-Konasana, 161-162
Spine:
  keeping flexible, exercises for:
    Angular Rest pose, 161-162
    Camel posture, 95-96
    Plough posture, 93-94
    Rocking, 17-19
    Wood-chopping movement, 148
  keeping straight, importance of, 9-10
  strengthening, exercises for:
    Swan posture, 114-116
    Twist posture, 116-118, 142-143, 163-165
Spirit and Matter, divine marriage of, 132-133
Spleen troubles, exercises for:
  Angular Rest pose, 161-162
  Churning pose, 121-123
  Headstand, 85-91, 112-114, 137-141
  Head-to-Knee posture, 21-23
  Plough posture, 93-94
  Shoulderstand, 143-145
  Twist posture, 116-118, 142-143, 163-165
Squatting pose, 29-32
  benefits of, 31
  common use of in Orient, 29
  (ill.), 30
  technique, 29-31

Index

Starch:
  digestion of, 182
  in diet, 73, 81
  foods containing, 183-184
Steadiness exercises, 57
Stiffness, exercises for overcoming:
  on awaking, 17-19
  general, 93-94, 161-162
  knees, 29-32
Stimulants, 78, 80
Stomach, strengthening, exercise for, 145-147
Stomach Lift (see Abdominal Lift)
Stoop exercise, 50-53
Stork (see Footlift pose)
Story of the Adaptation Syndrome, The, Selye, 108
Stress, *defined,* 108
Stress of Life, Selye, 108
Stressors, *defined,* 108
Stretching exercise at waking-up, 3, 47
Stretching posture, 27, 91-93
  benefits of, 91
  caution, 91-93
  (ill.), 92
  technique, 91
  time, 91
Sugar, white vs. brown, 74-75
Supine Pelvic posture, 146
Supine posture, 145-147
  benefits of, 147
  (ill.), 146
  technique, 146
  time, 146
Svadishthara chakra, 131
Swanasana, 114-116
Swan posture, 114-116
  benefits of, 116
  (ill.), 115
  technique, 114-116
  time, 116
Swanson, Gloria, 26, 56-57
Swastikāsana, 9, 66
Symbol of Yoga exercise, 50-53
Symmetrical Pose, 66
Sympathetic nerves, exercise for, 27-29
System, cleaning out, 36-37, 42, 82

Tea, 80
Teenagers, malnutrition of, 70
Teeth:
  foods detrimental to, 75, 76
  hygiene of, 36

Tension:
  neuro-muscular, 102-104
  treatment of, 104-109
  overcoming, exercise for, 85-91, 112-114, 137-141
Thinking, power of positive and negative, 173-174
Thought-projection, 173
Throat:
  congested, exercise for, 85-91, 112-114, 137-141
  massaging and strengthening exercises:
    Lion posture, 96-98
    Swan posture, 114-116
Thymus gland, 107
Thyroid gland:
  exercises beneficial for:
    Angular Rest pose, 161-162
    Camel posture, 95-96
    Headstand, 85-91, 112-114, 137-141
    Plough posture, 93-94
    Reverse posture, 57-59
    Shoulderstand, 143-145
    Supine pose, 145-147
  function of, 107
  location of, 107
Toe-twisting exercise, 47-48
Tongue, color of, 4
Totney, Frank, 41
Toxic waste matter, eliminating, 36-37, 42
Triangle pose, 141-142
  (ill.), 141
  technique, 141
  time, 141-142
Triveni, 132
Truth about self, finding, 153-157
Twist posture, 27
  benefits of, 117-118
  first movement, 116-118
  (ill.), 117
  technique, 116-117
  time, 117
  second movement, 142-143
  (ill.), 142
  technique, 143
  time, 143
  third movement, 163-165
  (ill.), 164

Uddyiana Bandha, 27, 118-121
Udhitta Padāsana, 19-21

United Press, 69
Universal consciousness, merger with, 132, 134
Upanishad, Yogabija, 137
Ustrāsana, 95-96
Uterine troubles, exercise recommended for, 27-29
Utkāsana, 29-32

Vegetable juices, 80
Vegetables, 74, 77, 78, 81
Viparitakarani Mudra, 57-59
Vision, improving:
  through eye exercises, 14-16
  through neck exercises, 14
Visuddha chakra, 132
Vitality, increasing, exercises for:
  Bending-Forward posture, 54-55
  Headstand, 85-91, 112-114, 137-141
  Head-to-Knee posture, 21-23
  Recharging Breath, 147
  Revise posture, 57-59
  Wood-Chopping movement, 148
Vioekananda, Swami, 128
Volksgesundheit magazine, 76, 77

Waistline, sagging, exercise for, 59-63
Waking-up routine, 3-4, 47-48
Walking Breathing exercise, 100-101
Waste matter, toxic, eliminating, 36-37, 42
Water, drinking, 36-37, 42, 79-80
  iced, 79
Wilhelmj, C. M., 70
Wood-Chopping movement, 148
  (ill.), 149
Wrists, exercise for strengthening, 114-116

Yama, 150, 152-153
Yoga:
  code of morals, 150
  fields touched by, 38
  infiltration of into Western health practices, 120
Yoga, Fuller, 135
Yoga, Practical Guide for Students of, Sivananda, 175
Yoga Aphorisms, Patanjali, 169
Yoga Mudra, 27, 50-53
  benefits of, 51
  caution, 51-53
  (ill.), 52
  technique, 51
  time, 51

9 780548 444238

CPSIA information can be obtained at www.ICGtesting.com
Printed in the USA
BVOW05*0102060915

416751BV00006B/127/P